Praise for *Live ABOVE the Chaos*

"From near and far I've watched Laurie live out what is written in this book. Even when life is hard as nails, she responds by loving God and people. Laurie's style is personal and engaging, but know that she is also authentic and credible."

—Jewl Westphalen

Freedom in Christ Ministries, Knoxville, Tennessee

"Don't be deceived by the book's title. This book is not meant to 'help' you; it is meant to change your life and the lives of those you touch. Jesus *shows* the way for each of us to *Live ABOVE the Chaos* with strong and beautiful lives. I met Laurie over three decades ago as I began my freshman year in college. She *showed* me Jesus as she took me under her wing in a mentor relationship. Through this book, she continues to show me Jesus. Read this book. Ingest it. Do it. Your life and the lives of those around you will never be the same!"

—LeAnn Bonzo

MA Intercultural Studies, concentration in biblical and religious studies, Columbia International University

"Get ready. *Live ABOVE the Chaos* will challenge you to change! The author masterfully presents an insightful perspective on the brevity of life. The larger message, however, lies in explaining eternal perspective and changes you can make today that will strengthen your walk and embolden you to share your faith. The author lives out every word written. I know this because next to salvation, she is my greatest gift from God. Laurie is my wife."

—John O'Connor

Laurie's husband since August 14, 1993

Live ABOVE the Chaos

Dear Ken and Janice,
Ever since I was a little girl, you
have loved me and cheered me on. Thank
you for helping me get this book published.
I pray God blesses you with something within these
pages. I love you dearly.
Laurie M Connor
11.29.2014

Live ABOVE the Chaos

Display God's Strength and Beauty
No Matter What

Laurie O'Connor

10 9 8 7 6 5 4 3 2 1 1 1 8 1 4

ISBN: 978-0-9906625-7-0

Printed in the United States of America

Back cover photo taken by Caron Stajduhar

♾ This paper meets the requirements of ANSI/NISO Z39.48-1992 (Permanence of Paper)

This book is dedicated to my brother, Daniel Clay Thompson.

God used the tragedy of your death to
dismantle my weak faith.

He then carefully and lovingly
rebuilt it from the ground up to be
stronger and more beautiful than before.

Who I am today is largely connected to what
God has done in me through saying good-bye to you.

I still love you and miss you every day.

Part Five of this book,
People: How Do We Get All of This Loving Done?, is
dedicated to Ron and Marcia Pershall.

Because of your example and ministry through Action-Impact,
I was taught to care about people's souls.

Contents

Acknowledgments xi

Part One
Living IN the Chaos

Chapter One: Inspiration to Face the Chaos 3
Chapter Two: Laurie's Story 9

Part Two
Living ABOVE the Chaos

Chapter Three: Questions Answered 25

Why did Dan die early? 26
Why is God not to blame for Dan's death? 29
Why did "the curse" happen to all people? 35
Why did Jesus have to die? 39
Why did God give us choice? 43
Who is Satan? 45
Why is Satan permitted to operate today? 49
How is God in control of this chaos? 51
What decision faces each of us? 62

Why are we here? 67
Wrapping up the big questions 71

Chapter Four: Are You Living ABOVE the Chaos or IN It? 73

Part Three
Perspective: How Should We View Our Lives?

Chapter Five: As a Firework 81
Chapter Six: As a Picture Frame 95
Chapter Seven: As a Mathematician 103
Chapter Eight: As a Soldier 109
Chapter Nine: As a Space Maker 119
Chapter Ten: Is Our Perspective ABOVE the Chaos or IN It? 129

Part Four
Process: How Do We Live With a Clean Heart?

Chapter Eleven: Beginning the Process of Living with a Clean Heart 139
Chapter Twelve: Inviting the Holy Spirit to Take Over Our Hearts 153
Chapter Thirteen: Confessing Everything God Shows Us 167
Chapter Fourteen: Doing Everything You Know to Do 183
Chapter Fifteen: Is Our Process ABOVE the Chaos or IN It? 197

Part Five
People: How Do We Get All of This Loving Done?

Chapter Sixteen: Preparing to Love Everyone with God's Love 205

Chapter Seventeen:	Loving Children	215
Chapter Eighteen:	Loving Husbands	227
Chapter Nineteen:	Loving While Waiting for Marriage	237
Chapter Twenty:	Loving People Who Know Christ Already	241
Chapter Twenty-One:	Loving People Who Don't Yet Know Christ	247
Chapter Twenty-Two:	Prioritizing People	267
Chapter Twenty-Three:	Are Our People Priorities ABOVE the Chaos or IN It?	273
Chapter Twenty-Four:	It's Time to Rise Up and Shine!	277
Endnotes		285
About the Author		291

Acknowledgments

Over twelve years ago, I began to write a book, thinking I would finish it in one year. I didn't know about all the difficulties that would head my way and delay its completion. Maybe if I had known, I wouldn't have penned the first word. But now as I look back on the years, I find myself incredibly grateful to God. He was with me through each difficult circumstance, and He helped me write each word of this book, even while surrounded by chaos. I have felt as if He was making certain I was living out the title before allowing me to see this manuscript in print.

I initially invited twelve women to become involved with this book project by reading drafts and offering feedback. Most of you have understandably moved on with your lives. Three women remain on the team as I cross the finish line: Tish Beall, Sue Dillon, and Monica Scheidt. I thank these faithful friends for still believing in what God has done in me. In addition, I am indebted to Steve Brown, Karen Gilden, Lisa Herring, and Dianne Stavropoulos who helped edit later versions of the manuscript. Prior to final editing, LeAnn Bonzo provided significant assistance with her keen eye for clarifying meaning, simplifying the text, and critiquing for biblical correctness. From our college years until now—still friends. Thank you.

Margee Curran, you were unable to work on the book because of distance, but God uses your cheerleading role in my life and the safety of our intimate friendship to bolster my spirits and keep me believing that Jesus looks beautiful in me too.

I want to thank Ron and Marcia Pershall for their lifelong dedication to students who live in and around their home in Elverson, Pennsylvania. The seeds of truth you planted in me never left my heart even in the darkest times. You are responsible for cultivating my passion for people's souls.

I am grateful to certain people and ministries that have shaped me into the woman I am today. Significant pastors over the years include Willard Petrie, Rick Statham, John Rowell, and Andy Stanley. My life has been changed through the Bible Study materials and books written by Henry Blackaby, Steve Estes, Josh McDowell, Beth Moore, and Joni Eareckson Tada. The work of Freedom in Christ Ministries and my friendship with Jewl Westphalen and her family are priceless. More recently, I have been challenged by Ann Voskamp, David Platt, Francis Chan, and Crawford Loritts. To all, your fingerprints appear throughout this book because you have influenced my life.

Mom, thank you for taking me to church every Sunday during my childhood. Because of your faithfulness, I enjoyed long-term, influential relationships with amazing church families and was able to respond to God's love and become a follower of Christ.

Dad, you love me just the way I am, totally and completely. Thank you for picking up the phone so consistently and talking so openly. No daughter loves her father more.

David, you and I both lost our brother, Dan. I hope that reading about my healing process assists you with yours. I love you.

Caitlin and Callie, you are a double joy, arriving as my daughters on the same day. You couldn't be more different from each other, but both of you are beautiful, talented, athletic, studious, and kind. Thank you for doing household chores and babysitting your younger brother over the years so I could write. Now that you are in college, may you reap the full reward for such discipline and unending devotion to your mom.

Clay, I wanted another child and have no idea why God had me wait ten years to get you. You are a delight, a prize, a gift, a joy. You are my boy. Through your adoption, I have a deeper understanding of what salvation means—an all-out rescue initiated and carried out by God alone. May you live out your name and the life verse we have selected for you: 2 Corinthians 4:7.

Zoe, some of my most precious memories include watching God orchestrate your adoption and getting you safely into the arms of your mom and dad. I will love you always.

Elizabeth, Jack, Terra, and Nick, thank you for participating in a relationship with your stepmother. You didn't have to give me a chance. I love each of you for that decision.

I save the most important person for last, the dad of seven (so far). Thank you, John. We lived the events of the last thirteen book-writing years arm-in-arm. This journey got long, but no matter how difficult our circumstances became, no matter how thin our finances got, your voice always said, "Keep writing." Thank you for letting me share so much of our story in this book. You didn't have to choose vulnerability, and I believe the book is better for it. I wouldn't want to be doing this thing called life with anyone else but you.

Part One

Living IN the Chaos

Chapter One

Inspiration to Face the Chaos

Life is messy

Life is messy for all of us, isn't it? Relationships, health, finances, job pressures or unemployment, marriage, perhaps divorce, children—all of these complicate our lives. The list never ends.

My husband and I have a blended family of seven children (four from his previous marriage and three from our marriage). I teach communication courses at a local college where I interact with approximately 250 students each year. Because of the number of lives touching mine, life surprises me by the minute. When I add in social obligations, athletic activities, school events, home maintenance, finances, and medical concerns, my days are full, just like yours.

What follows is a collection of memorable sentences, both happy and sad, that have been a part of my chaos:

- "Dan has been in a motorcycle accident and is not expected to live through the night."

- "John, we are having twins!"
- "I am sorry, ma'am, your debit card is denied."
- "Your siding is infested with carpenter bees and your septic system has failed." (This was said on a day there was no money to pay for either.)
- "Honey, we need to go to court with this matter."
- A daughter announces, "Mom and Dad, I am pregnant and want to get married."
- An extended family member calls and says, "I would like you to adopt my son."
- "There will be eleven around the Christmas tree this year!"
- "Laurie, I am going to retire and start a new business."
- "You do not qualify for refinancing. I am sorry."
- "Laurie, your daughter has an autoimmune disease like you."

As if this list of heart-stopping sentences isn't enough, it's tossed together with the types of sentences familiar to us all:

- "Mom, where are my soccer socks?" (Minutes before leaving for the soccer game.)
- "Mom, the band concert is the same night as our game!"
- "Mom, I feel like I am going to throw up."
- "There's no more dog food!"
- "Mom, my hamster died!"

All of these circumstances can tumble together for heightened drama. Like the day when one daughter is ecstatic because she was asked to the prom, while the other one is sobbing in her bedroom because she hasn't yet been asked. Like the day when one daughter has the soccer game of her life and scores three goals against a team ranked thirteenth in the nation, while in the same match the other daughter is falsely accused of a foul in a game-changing play. Or how about the Thanksgiving Day our home is buzzing with excitement because our oldest daughter and family are just a few miles away; then, BAM, we hear the giant spring on our garage door spontaneously snap in two? Sometimes I feel like a pinball being hit from one paddle to another, never knowing in what direction I will be ricocheted next.

I know I am not alone. That's why you picked up this book.

Life is just plain hard, isn't it? For years I didn't understand the chaos around me, so I let it confuse and defeat me. Quite frankly, I gave up for a season and made a mess of my life. I know I am not alone in that either. There are women (and men) like me all around the globe.

I would like to encourage you with the message of this book: chaos does not have to overtake you. You can live above it by seeing the chaos in proper *perspective*; participating in the *process* God uses to grow you, and loving the *people* in your life with God's love.

By the end of this book, I hope you see clearly that your existence is larger than what occupies your time—complicated family schedules, job responsibilities, household duties, school assignments, athletic activities, hobbies, and volunteer service. The greater reality of your life is about God—what He is doing *around* you, *in* you, *for* you, and *through* you.

At any moment, one of my chaos-inducing sentences may become one of yours and one of your sentences may become mine, but we meet on the common ground that life is difficult for each of us. Chaos doesn't have to disqualify us from living strong and beautiful lives. God wants us to look back at the end of our lives and see that we lived for purposes beyond the dot of time and space we occupy on history's timeline. He wants our lives to count for eternity, and they can—*no matter what.*

Why this book? Why listen to me?

There was a day in my past when a catastrophic event blew my life apart and shattered my faith in God. For seven years after that fateful autumn day, I responded to the pain in a way that did absolutely nothing except produce a self-created mess to clean up. Slowly but surely, God brought me out of the pit of pain and despair, one step at a time.

I can't be the only woman who has discovered her faith was weak. Perhaps what I have learned on my journey back to a healthier relationship with God will help you make some sense out of the turbulent parts of your life. Some of the troubles I have experienced are my fault, and others have been imposed upon me. But I can say today that though the chaos of life is still present every moment, I love Jesus more than I ever have. The world makes more sense to me now. I invite you to begin a journey to bravely look at how chaos affects you, and then come out on the other side as a person less rocked by your circumstances.

As a result of the hard lessons I have learned from my spiritual detour, a dream wells up within me. I desire for *every Christian around the world* to reflect the character of Christ, both individually and corporately. Jesus said, "You are the light of the world . . ." (Matthew 5:14). My heart desires that Christians join forces so they can light up the world:

- with an *attractive* light—one that is worthy of His name (Matthew 5:16);

- with a *strong* light—one that continues to shine regardless of the circumstances (Philippians 1:27);
- and with a *productive life*—one that invests in people (2 Timothy 2:2).

Is there a part of you that wants to rise up and live a life like this? Or do you have a hard time believing you can get there from where you are today? Travel with me through the pages of this book and learn about my journey back to God. My hope is that you will be inspired, refreshed, and will gain the courage to believe that you can be strong and beautiful too.

Chapter Two

Laurie's Story

From the beginning

It will be impossible for you to understand how much I lost my way unless you understand a little bit about where I came from. I have no idea why, but I had the opportunity to learn about how to have a personal relationship with Jesus at the age of twelve. It happened one Friday night when my church youth group visited a high school ministry called Action-Impact. Students were meeting in the basement of a home in Malvern, Pennsylvania, and one young man asked if he could talk to me about how to have a personal relationship with Jesus. I think his name was Tim. We were standing together in a hallway where people could see us, so I was cognizant of wanting to look "cool." I leaned against the wall with my arms across my chest and responded to his questions with answers like, "Oh, I know that . . . I understand . . . I've heard that before." Despite my nonchalance, he told me about a way I could be certain I was going to heaven.

When Tim went home that night, he was probably disappointed about how I had responded to the gentle and succinct message he had offered. He does not yet know what God did with the seeds that were planted in my heart that night. The following Thursday, my mom and I were leaving the house to go to our church choir practice together when the phone rang. She went back inside the house to answer. I sat on the front stoop and had time to act upon what I had been mulling over in my mind ever since Tim had explained I could be certain that I was going to heaven. I had never known certainty was possible. I had also never understood that the way to gain that certainty—confidence of a life in heaven after death—was to trust Jesus for the forgiveness of my sins.

The stars glistened against the black canopy of sky that night. Our home's outside lighting reflected off the maple tree next to the mailbox. My feet were resting on the stone walk leading to our front door. I was memorizing the scene on purpose because I was on the verge of a big moment, and I never wanted to forget it. As best as I knew how, I was giving my life to Jesus because He had died for me. My prayer began with, "God, I want to memorize this night because I never want to forget that here and now I am placing my faith for the forgiveness of my sins in Jesus Christ alone. I do not trust in myself or anything else to get to heaven . . . just the cross alone . . . just Jesus paying for my sins by dying for them."

I never again saw the young man who cared enough to tell me about Jesus. I will squeal with delight when I hug him in heaven . . . and confirm his name! Action-Impact moved its location near my home, so I continued to be involved in that ministry. During my middle and high school years, I followed Tim's example, and talked with people about how to know Jesus. While attending a university in Pennsylvania, I spent some summers on mission trips to stateside beaches and third-world countries. When I graduated, I decided to enter full-time Christian work on college campuses. I probably appeared at that time to be a woman who loved Jesus Christ and had strong faith. Half of that was true. I loved Jesus Christ. What I didn't know at the time was that my faith was anything but strong.

Chaos strikes

I woke up on a beautiful Saturday morning in October of 1986 as a twenty-five-year-old graduate student living in Maryland. The crimson, golden, and russet leaves beckoned me outdoors for my weekly run with school friends at a nearby park. I returned invigorated from filling my lungs with crisp autumn air while enjoying the crunch of dry leaves underfoot on the wooded running path. The house I shared with a single mother and her son was empty when I returned home, so I took my time showering, donned my favorite sweats, and settled in for an afternoon of studying.

Please allow me to underline the fact that I was happy that day. I had cleaned my entire room the night before so I was feeling organized, healthy, productive, and *in control.* Even the weather was cooperating with me! As embarrassing as it is to admit now, I remember thinking, *Wow, I have the formula for a successful life down pat.*

Then the phone rang.

I got up from my desk and walked across the long basement room to the phone on the wall.

"Laurie?" It was my mom. She was crying and her voice was shaky and strained. To this day, the words are a blur; I just remember the devastating news that rocked my world. My dear brother, Dan, had been struck by a car while riding his motorcycle in his neighborhood. He was twenty-three. Mom explained that he was not expected to live through the night. She asked that I pack my bags and drive immediately from Maryland to a hospital in New Jersey where Dan lay in intensive care.

So grateful to be alone, I stumbled through the house screaming, "Nooooooo!" at the top of my lungs . . . over and over again. Finally, falling on my knees in the living room, I collapsed against an end table and soaked the sleeves of my favorite sweatshirt with tears. The walls of that tiny living room remain the only witness to my first soul-wrenching sobs that day.

Dan had possessed a jovial, life-of-the-party personality wrapped up in a huge football-playing body. He had played football his first three years of college at a Pennsylvania university but had taken his senior year off to give his hip, which had been causing him chronic pain, a chance to heal. He ended up finding work in New Jersey, so he moved to the Jersey Shore.

One by one, my family members traveled from Pennsylvania to the hospital. My younger, twenty-one-year-old brother, David, had arrived first, followed by my parents. Because of my distress, I asked my friend, LeAnn, to drive me to the hospital from Maryland. We were the last to arrive.

We began to put the pieces together about how the accident had happened. My brother had been fixing his motorcycle and taking test drives—down a few blocks and then back. On one of those spins, a man pulled out in his car from a side street and into my brother's path. The collision sent Dan soaring through the air. His muscular body could not compete with the impact against rock-hard pavement. He became immediately unconscious before slipping into a coma.

Over the next week, my family members and I took turns at Dan's bedside. The nurses explained that hearing is the last of our senses to go; so, when it was my turn to sit at Dan's bedside, I never stopped talking. I recounted every memory that came to mind and said, "I love you," a thousand times. One tragic evening, in an effort to correct his electrolytes, fluid was added to Dan's body. Every drop went to his brain and caused swelling. Throughout the night, my brother progressively lost brain function and slowly died. He was pronounced brain-dead by morning, eight days after his accident.

Since Dan was healthy when he died and was still connected to life support, we were asked about donating his organs. We agreed that if we couldn't have Dan any longer, at least some good would come from extending life to others.

I heard later that one of my brother's best friends, Patsy, had said, "Whoever gets Dan's heart is getting a really big heart." Dan had been known to lend the living room couch out to anyone who needed it. His roommates joked that they never knew which of his buddies would be in the house when they got up in the morning.

After the decision was made to donate Dan's organs, we took turns entering his curtained sanctum to say good-bye. Dan was still on life support until organ recipients could be found, so his body was still "alive." I laid my head on his chest and memorized the sound of his heartbeat and the steadiness of his machine-governed breathing. I inhaled deeply to remember how his skin smelled. Then I kissed my brother on the cheek for the last time and left the hospital without him.

I will never forget the silent drive home as my family traveled from the Jersey Shore to my parents' Pennsylvania home. As Mom and I walked toward the front door, she was greeted by our dog, Holly. Mom bent over to pat her head and said, "Danny isn't coming home." That night, none of us could imagine laughing again or enjoying a meal without Dan at the table with us.

The funeral was standing room only, leaving me with memories of certain people, particular flower arrangements, and distinct sentences spoken about Dan. As part of my grieving, I spent time making a photomontage of Dan's life on four large poster boards. I displayed these prominently at the viewing and funeral so visitors could get to know more about his entire lifetime, not just the segment in which they knew him. As I assembled them, I kept expecting Dan to show up and tell me how great the display looked.

The long day ended. Our family placed roses on his casket, and it was lowered into the ground. The crowd dispersed. Then life demanded an amazing feat from me—to move on without Dan. Somehow, our entire family had to figure out how to create a new sense of togetherness around a giant, black hole that now existed between us, the space my beloved brother once occupied. I drove back to graduate school, and continued to attend classes and teach communication courses, but my heart remained a gaping wound.

Chaos takes control

Dan's death could not have occurred at a worse time for me. During the year prior to his death, we had reconnected as adults. We had been talking every weekend by phone and pulling all-nighters when we saw each other in person, eager to talk about the details of our lives. I couldn't believe that after all I had done for God in the form of a good life and service, He had taken my brother. I was crushed. Hope died within me—the hope that if I lived a certain way, things would go my way. I no longer felt any sense of control over my destiny. I felt like God didn't love me any longer. My logic went like this: if God can turn on me then I must not be worthy of His love, or He must not be worthy of mine. Something inside of me gave up, and that departure from living fervently for God lasted seven years.

During those years, my shattered heart and confused picture of God led me to make poor decisions that pushed me further into chaos and away from the life I had always lived. If someone had pointed toward me during those years and said to you, "When she was twelve, she made a decision to trust Jesus as her Savior," you would have exclaimed, "No way!" My mouth regularly spewed profanity, and I began frequently drinking alcohol in excess. The most marked difference in my lifestyle, however, was with how I related to men.

One of those relationships included a marriage and then a divorce. I am the one who left the marriage after our fourth wedding anniversary. I loved my first husband, but I was unable to break through my own pain and dysfunction in order to accept and enjoy him the way he deserved.

Following my divorce, I had a string of dating relationships with men I had no business spending time with. Desperation had set in. Was there anyone out there who would love me? I worked really hard at being a good date and then a good girlfriend. The hardworking gal I had always been never completely went away. She was still inside of me, now striving to find a man who would love her back. No matter how hard I tried, the relationships ended abruptly with quick phone calls and sentences that hang in my memory like, "This just isn't fun for me anymore." Spinning, striving, trying—and getting nowhere fast. That was me.

As crazy as it sounds, while my personal life was in shambles, I was excelling in my career as a businesswoman, and was re-located to Georgia. My daily commute was lengthy. I remember doing some thinking on a late night trip home and spontaneously yelling to God, "You aren't going to let me have a man are You?" I sensed God was up in the sky limiting the level of disaster I was creating for myself by not allowing my destructive relationships to work out. I wondered if God was causing men to end their relationships with me since I wasn't willing to stop the relationships myself. Perhaps He hadn't forgotten about me after all.

I began a dating relationship with a man named John. During the first year we dated, several deaths or near deaths occurred among his coworkers. As John processed these intense experiences, he brought up the subject of life after death. I said, "I'm not living anything I am about to say, but I want you to know the truth about how someone goes to heaven." I then explained to John how Jesus came to die for our sins, and if we trust Christ's payment as our own, we can be assured of eternal life in heaven. Thanks to God and the faithful work done by Action-Impact, the truth of salvation miraculously never left the center of my soul, even in the midst of my rebellion and chaotic circumstances.

On the Easter Sunday about a year after John and I had met, I took an at-home pregnancy test and confirmed I was going to become a mother. I responded by curling up in my dry bathtub with my cheek pressed next to the drain. I allowed the tears to flow. I wasn't weeping about having a baby. I wept mostly because any hope of maintaining the façade that I was a capable businesswoman who had her life together was now shattered. I knew the destructive path on which I was careening had just come to an abrupt end. My tired soul was crying out, "Enough of this!" The sheer emotion of comprehending all the self-inflicted messes tumbled out of me. It's a good thing I was crying next to a bathtub drain!

My response to chaos changes

I know of no other way to put this. I got up from those humbling minutes in the bathtub a new woman. No more faking. No more lying. No more pretenses. I embraced honesty. I embraced change. I embraced God again. *If your life is a mess right now, understand something. God will take you back right this instant.* This comes from a woman who climbed out of a porcelain tub in 1993 and hasn't looked back since!

I found John pacing in the living room. After announcing the pregnancy, I put my hands against his chest and gently pushed him back far enough to look directly into his eyes.

"John, I am going back to God," I said. "This means I will be going to church again and will no longer be the girl you have been dating up until now. My language and behavior won't look anything like what you are used to—effective immediately. You are free to leave right now and never return. It's okay. I know you didn't bargain for this."

John stayed in spite of the changes, which included stopping all intimate physical contact. I meant business, and apparently he did too since he hung in there. John didn't know that in my heart I had also made another decision. I had decided that I would not marry him unless he became a Christian. The way I figured it, I had made enough destructive decisions and didn't need to compound things by marrying a man who couldn't share in my perspectives, heart motivations, and lifestyle. This decision remained private to make sure anything John did with regard to God was not connected to coercion on my part.

Three months went by. On Father's Day, John and I went to a little church we had been attending since the news of the pregnancy. I opened up the bulletin that morning and read that John was getting baptized. With a gaping mouth, I turned to see him smiling with deep satisfaction that he'd kept the secret.

It turned out the crisis of my pregnancy caused him to consider his relationship with God as well. John had gone running on wooded trails that week and at some point, he stood still and trusted Christ as his Savior. Wanting to surprise me, he arranged to be baptized right away as a public declaration of his decision, and that's when I found out.

I couldn't believe what had transpired. It felt like the God of the universe had just reached down through the clouds with His mighty right arm and rescued me. I took John's decision to trust Christ to mean I could marry him with a clear conscience. I did not have to be a single mom, though that is exactly what I had determined to be were it not for this miraculous turn of events.

John and I married quickly because the pregnancy was past midpoint already. My sweet father escorted a bride who was five and a half months pregnant—with twins! No bride was happier.

John and I moved into our first home, and began married life in a rush. Our sweet twin girls arrived six and a half weeks earlier than planned. Getting their premature, little bodies through their first few months of life consumed us. During quiet minutes at night, however, or during random hours of the day when they were both napping and John was at work, I felt a tug at my soul. I absolutely knew the greater priority of my life was to get my spiritual life together. I was very disconcerted that all it had taken was one tragedy to send me on a path of self-destruction and to living a life diametrically opposed to the kind of life I had always lived. *If nothing else, I wanted to become a woman strong enough to live well no matter what happened around me.*

Starting over

When the calendar turned to a new year in my second marriage, it was time to look in the mirror and face what I had done. How does a girl become a Christian, do all the "right" things, love God dearly, serve Him wholeheartedly, and then fall apart when tragedy strikes? I knew if I didn't figure this out, I would spend my life living with the fear that I could be knocked down by the next tough circumstance that came my way. I couldn't live like that!

> The one who received the seed that fell on rocky places is the man who hears the word and receives it with joy. But since he has no root, he lasts only a short time. When trouble or persecution comes because of the word, he quickly falls away.
>
> —Matthew 13:20–21

You might as well insert my name in the parable: The one who received the seed that fell on rocky places is like Laurie who heard the Word and at once received it with joy. But since she had no root, she lasted only a short time. When her brother died and life didn't go her way, she quickly fell away.

I stood up that New Year's Day, dusted myself off, and asked God to take me on a journey back into my past to sort out what had gone wrong and to transform me into a woman who really *is* strong, and doesn't just look the part. God has since revealed several reasons why I was not deeply rooted, and was unable to handle a major storm without being pushed over.

> ***Reason #1:*** I did not understand my sinfulness in the presence of a holy God.
>
> Truth be told, I thought God was getting a great deal when I became a Christian, since I was going to do a lot for Him. It took some time to realize that I can do nothing of eternal value apart from God.

> ***Reason #2:*** I had a subconscious "deal" with God.
>
> The deal was, "If I do all this for You, God, You don't touch my brother or anything else extremely valuable to me." Contributing to the searing pain caused by Dan's death was the sense of betrayal that God had broken His end of our "bargain." Simply put, my relationship with God had begun with strings attached to it. I didn't know how safe and loving God was, so I had never *really* trusted Him.

> ***Reason #3:*** I was trying to earn God's love.
>
> My relationship with God was based on striving hard to earn God's love rather than relaxing in the reality that God already fully loved me. I cannot earn more of His love. I had foolishly grabbed a "to-do" list of what a good

Christian looks like, and was tackling it with all the gusto I could muster so God would be proud of me. Truth is, I was exhausted by trying to live the Christian life based on an overestimation of myself and my abilities, deals with God, and relentless work.

Reason #4: I was more interested in going to heaven than knowing God.

It would take years to figure out, but when I prayed to receive Christ as my Savior, my decision was more about gaining heaven than allowing Christ to also be my Lord.

As I began to understand these four reasons as to why I had not been deeply rooted in God, I started to journey with God the second time around with a large dose of humility and a clearer understanding that I had a lot to learn. Today, I live with greater confidence that God's perfect love for me is never at stake. On the outside, I probably look as industrious as I did then, but now on the inside, I am not striving feverishly to keep the world spinning. God can do that all by Himself!

As I look back, I see that God never stopped pursuing me between the time I departed from Him and the time He got me back on an Easter Sunday while crying tears into a drain. God never let me go. I believe there's a chance He let my response to Dan's death play out within the safe confines of His love, so I could fully realize my deep need for Him.

During my descent into chaos, I believed Christ was my Savior. But I did not understand that establishing a relationship with God through Jesus involves more than praying a prayer—or for that matter attending church, being baptized, or taking communion. Jesus calls us to follow Him. Plain and simple. To be a Christian really means to be a Christ follower. This is what I needed to understand in order to become, and to remain, strong and beautiful in Him.

Ever since I came to my senses and asked for answers, God has been teaching me how to consistently grow in my ability to live ABOVE the chaos, rather than being controlled by it. In more ways than one, I have celebrated the Easter Day I hit bottom near a bathtub drain as a Resurrection Day.

Part Two

Living ABOVE the Chaos

Chapter Three

Questions Answered

I heard a story about a man whose children were misbehaving on an airplane. Nearby passengers expressed their displeasure by glaring and muttering. The tired father of the unruly children said apologetically, "I am sorry my children aren't themselves. We are returning from their mother's funeral." Suddenly, passengers were eager to engage with the children by entertaining them, feeding them snacks, and holding them when cranky. Perspective makes all the difference. Examining the context surrounding any situation provides insight that almost never fails to influence our responses.

I feel as if something has been lost in the church within my generation, at least in America. It feels like people have picked up bits and pieces of teaching here and there but do not have a larger framework on which to hang the knowledge. Answers to big questions are brief and inadequate at best, and the answers aren't connecting to a larger cohesive story. As I reflected on my messed up life, I knew that part of the reason I had responded poorly to Dan's death was because I had understood neither the historical nor spiritual context surrounding my life.

Below are key questions and answers that have provided the context that has changed my responses to life in general, and to chaos and troubles specifically. I have learned I am not the only one who has missed a proper introduction to contextual concepts. I hope these answers to my specific questions, as well as to common inquiries, begin to anchor your soul amid the waves of surprises, troubles, and changes that attempt to overtake each of us.

Why did Dan die early?

> Man is like a breath; his days are like a fleeting shadow.
>
> —Psalm 144:4

I am extremely analytical. You may not be, but please try to hang in there with me about how to view life as *short.* If you can grapple with this to the point of comprehending life's brevity, the ensuing perspectives can be life-changing.

Look around your home right now—or wherever you are reading—and imagine string wound around every item in the room. String is everywhere. Now in your mind's eye, make a dot on that string . . . one tiny dot. Continue to imagine now stepping some distance away from the dot on the string. You will no longer be able to see the tiny dot though it will still be *fully present* amidst all that tangled string.

The string represents eternity, and the dot represents how short your life span is compared to eternity. The length of your life shrinks in comparison to that massive length of string. Compared to "forever" our life spans are a pinpoint, a speck, a snap of the fingers, the quick breath it takes to blow out a birthday candle. Concentrate on the next blink of your eyes.

The length of your life will pass by as quickly as a blink when compared to the length of eternity (Psalm 103:13–16).

Please look to the following page right now to view the concept we have been imagining.

It's this dot-on-a-string idea that eventually allowed me to grasp the fact that Dan didn't die early. Let's keep working with this concept and hone in on the dot as a life span. Imagine in your mind's eye that the dot on the string, or the period at the end of this sentence is comprised of eighty microscopic pieces clumped together. These pieces represent eighty years. Now, try to imagine making a pile of only twenty-three of these tiny pieces. These represent the length of Dan's life. Now, compare the two piles.

With the naked eye, there appears to be no measurable difference between the twenty-three tiny pieces and the eighty tiny pieces. Dan did not die earlier than I—not really—when I view human lives in light of eternity and as dots on a string. Compared to "forever," my life is as brief as Dan's life was. Both of our existences are mere breaths. Allow me to gently say that compared to eternity, the wrinkled old lady does not live longer than the infant. In light of eternity, no one dies "early."

I don't want to sound glib to those of you reading this who have lost children, or have experienced any other similar horrific scenario. I understand that the pain of losing young children exceeds my pain of losing an adult brother. I really do. But let's not compare pain. Let's focus on the *truth* just presented.

ETERNITY

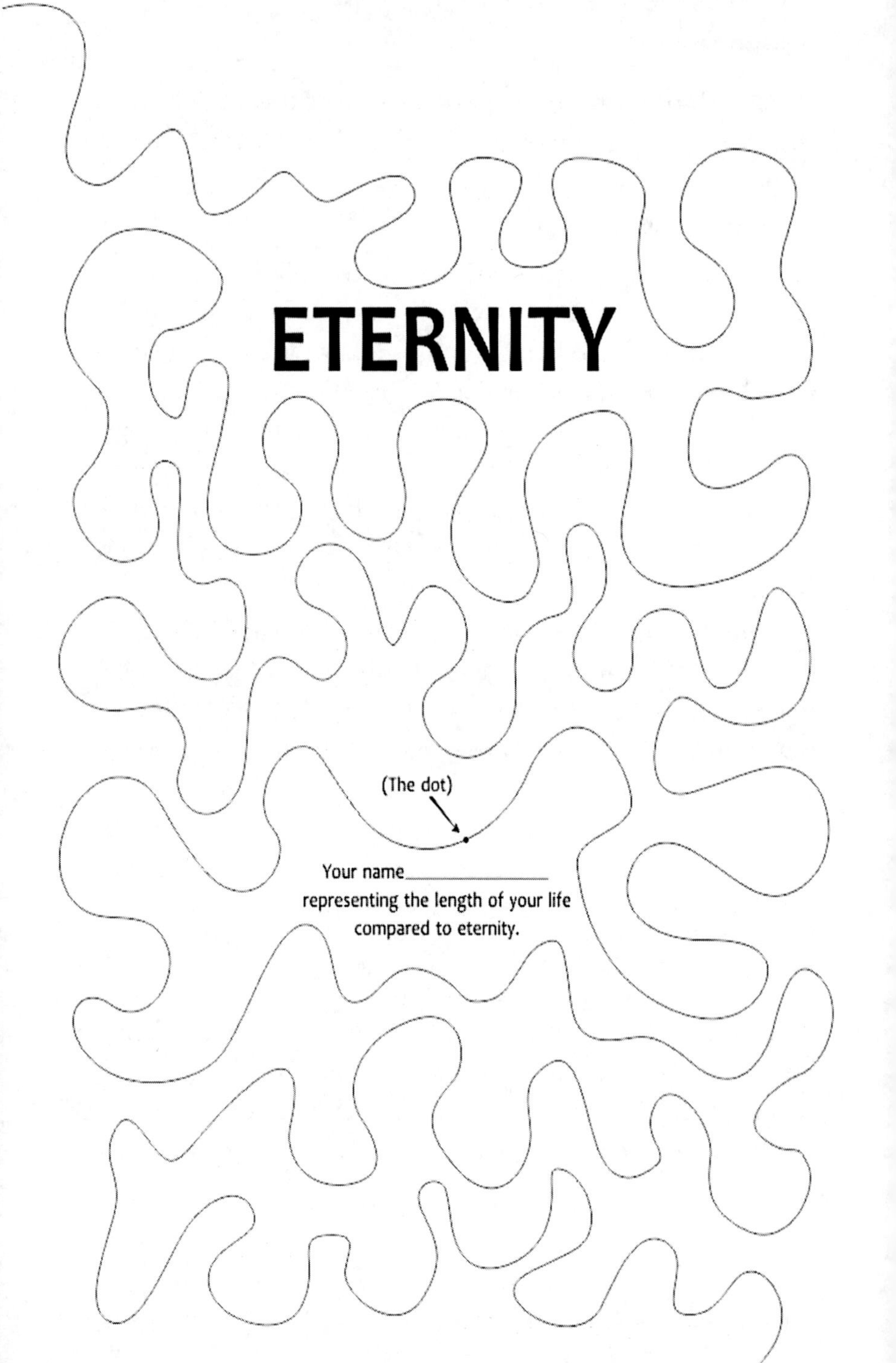

(The dot)

Your name________________
representing the length of your life
compared to eternity.

None of us can guess how we will respond to tragedy when it strikes. However, I know that if one of my children arrives in heaven before me, my friends will find me curled in a weepy mess grieving the loss of my precious young one. And I hope they will find me clutching a tear-soaked piece of paper with a tiny dot on it signifying that I am clinging to the truths that *all* lives are brief and that my child did *not* die early when compared to eternity.

For the remainder of this book, when I refer to the "dot" and the "string," I will be using them in this specific application: the dot represents anything that exists within a time frame and the string represents eternity. As the book unfolds, we will consider other things besides life spans that are represented by this dot.

Folks, even chaos has a beginning and an end. If our hearts can grasp that chaos is contained in a dot of time so small it is invisible to the naked eye, then true perspective can occur. *All* time frames become short from the vantage point of eternity, and *all* chaos is fleeting.

Why did Dan die early? He didn't. No one dies early when one sees each life span confined to a dot as compared to the string of eternity.

Why is God not to blame for Dan's death?

In order to comprehend why God is not to blame for Dan's death, I needed to understand more of God's heart. If you want to know about God's heart for all of us and what life is meant to be with Him, start with His original creation of earth and His original relationship with the first humans, Adam and Eve. We learn about God's desired plan for humanity in Genesis 1–3. We learn from these chapters that God created a world which would meet humanity's every need (Genesis 1). He planted a delightful garden, called Eden, filled with vegetation for eating and rivers for drinking (Genesis 2:8–14). From what we read in Genesis 2, this seemed to be a special place of habitation for Adam and Eve. God endowed this first couple with authority and responsibility (Genesis 1:28 and 2:15, 19–20). In addition, God gifted them with companionship (Genesis 2:18, 22–25). We can infer by what is written in Genesis 3:8–11 that until Eve and then Adam ate from the tree of the knowledge of good and evil, they enjoyed uninterrupted fellowship with God.

I could write this entire book on Genesis 1–3, but I don't have space to do so! What follows are some of the earthshattering parts that give me confidence God did not cause the accident that killed my brother.

The first confidence building part concerns the trees in the center of the garden of Eden. Amidst all the gifts God bestowed upon Adam and Eve, He gave only one rule (Genesis 2:16–17). Specifically, notice there were *two trees* in the middle of the garden of Eden, but only *one* rule about *one* tree:

Tree of Life

Tree of the Knowledge of Good and Evil

Two trees:

> Now the Lord God had planted a garden in the east, in Eden; and there he put the man he had formed . . . In the middle of the garden were the tree of life and the tree of the knowledge of good and evil.
>
> —Genesis 2:8–9

One rule about one tree:

> And the Lord God commanded the man, "You are free to eat from any tree in the garden; but you must not eat from the tree of the knowledge of good and evil, for when you eat of it you will surely die."
>
> —Genesis 2:16–17

I have heard questions about why God had to have any rules at all, but I remain stunned that there was only one rule! Before discussing the tree from which Adam and Eve could *not* eat, let's first celebrate the trees from which they *could* eat. In the garden of Eden, every tree was a "yes" and only one was "no." God provided evidence that He loves to say "yes!" by creating a world of immense freedom. Can we get excited about that? In addition to eating from every other tree in the garden, Adam and Eve were originally permitted to eat from the tree of life as well—the one that would allow them to live forever (Genesis 3:22)!

Life filled the garden of Eden. Death was nowhere to be found in the original world God set up for Adam and Eve. It was introduced when the serpent tempted Eve to eat from the tree of the knowledge of good and evil (Genesis 3:1–6).

Eve gets a bad rap for eating from the tree of the knowledge of good and evil and then passing the fruit to Adam who also ate (Genesis 3:6). She did indeed disobey the one rule God set up, but let's remember she did not have knowledge of evil. We, on the other hand, possess knowledge of evil. It is unfair to assess Adam or Eve's behavior through the lens of the knowledge-of-evil we now possess.

No analogy is perfect, but I liken Eve's encounter with Satan to that of a sexual predator approaching a child on a playground. The parents have told the child not to talk to strangers or go anywhere with strangers. If the child talks to or goes with a stranger, he or she has disobeyed her parents. But why aren't we angry at the child when we hear about an abduction? It's because children have no knowledge of this kind of evil. They receive the instruction about not talking to strangers without the accompanying knowledge of duct tape, car trunks, lewd acts, and murder. Such innocence leaves them vulnerable to being lured or tricked. The only enemy in the garden of Eden scenario was Satan, who was honing in on the vulnerable aspects of Eve through deception. She could not have imagined the evil that would be introduced by her disobedience, and neither could Adam. The same is true for you and me. The consequences of our decisions apart from a life-giving God are always much worse than we ever think they are going to be.

God not only gives life; He is life. To disconnect from life brings death. It is a principle that governs our lives. This was illustrated to my husband and me at the birth of our twin daughters. Our first daughter arrived safe and sound, squalling loudly and red-faced. While preparing to deliver our second daughter, the attending physician discovered her heart was barely beating. Our baby was fighting for her life inside my womb.

An emergency C-section took place right in the unsterile delivery room. Unlike the first daughter, our second daughter arrived still and blue. A medical team conducted artificial respiration for twenty-eight minutes, and thankfully, she is alive and well today. Doctors were able to ascertain that the placenta had disconnected from my body. My daughter had been floating around inside of me with no connection to a life source. Death occurs when there is no life source. Medical technology can blur the line between life and death by means of "life support," but in the natural world, the line is clear. God made Adam out of the dust of the ground and then breathed life into him (Genesis 2:7). God Himself was the source of life. Once Adam and Eve were no longer in intimate fellowship with God, they became spiritually dead.

In Genesis 3:13–19, we learn that along with spiritual death—separation from God—Adam and Eve were cursed with physical death, sickness, a struggle to earn a living, and the operative presence of the devil in the world. All of us who have been born since live under this same curse of spiritual death with all of its consequences. Collectively, this death and the consequences are referred to as "the curse."

Note God's fresh concern for the tree of life once Adam and Eve had eaten from the tree of the knowledge of good and evil.

> And the Lord God said, "The man has now become like one of us, knowing good and evil. He must not be allowed to reach out his hand and take also from the tree of life and eat, and live forever." So the Lord God banished him from the garden of Eden to work the ground from which he had been taken.
>
> —Genesis 3:22–23

I hear people talk about the harshness of God banning Adam and Eve from the garden of Eden. *If they had eaten from the tree of life in their state of broken relationship with God, however, life under the curse would have lasted forever.* Banning humanity from the garden of Eden protected the story of the string and kept chaos contained in a dot.[1] Our current broken world will *not* last forever. There is a plan in place for the full restoration of earth. God says, "Behold, I will create new heavens and a new earth. The former things will not be remembered, nor will they come to mind" (Isaiah 65:17).

Here's a glimpse of the end of time when God creates a new heaven and earth: Never again will there be an infant who lives but a few days or an old man who does not live out his years (Isaiah 65:20). There will be no untimely deaths ever again. There will be no more death, period (Revelation 21:4). And perhaps the most exciting thing is there will be no more curse (Revelation 22:3).

Guarded by cherubim and a flaming
sword flashing back and forth.

Tree of Life

This happy ending for history is being protected today. "After he drove the man out, he placed on the east side of the garden of Eden cherubim and a flaming sword flashing back and forth to guard the way to the tree of life" (Genesis 3:24). History is guarded and chaos contained because the tree of life is protected by cherubim, the angels responsible for guarding the holiness of God (Psalm 80:1, Psalm 99:1, Isaiah 37:16).[2] When this segment of history ends and the rest of eternity begins, we will freely eat from the tree of life again—without any curse!

> On each side of the river stood the tree of life, bearing twelve crops of fruit, each yielding its fruit each month. And the leaves of the tree are for the healing of the nations. No longer will there be any curse.
>
> —Revelation 22:2–3

God made Adam out of the dust of the ground and then breathed life into him (Genesis 2:7). God not only loves life; He *is* life. With these facts in mind, let's return to the question discussed in this section: *Why is God not to blame for Dan's death?* Death came with the curse. It did not originate from God. The *curse* killed Dan.

Why did "the curse" happen to all people?

"Holy, holy, holy is the Lord Almighty; the whole earth is full of his glory" (Isaiah 6:3).

Just like Eve gets a bad rap for eating from the tree of the knowledge of good and evil, and God gets misunderstood for banning Adam and Eve from the garden of Eden, God also gets questioned for instituting a curse upon all mankind. After both Eve and Adam ate from the tree, God cursed all three participants in the sin—the serpent, the woman, and the man (Genesis 3:14–

19). Look at the curse to Adam: "By the sweat of your brow you will eat your food until you return to the ground, since from it you were taken . . . for dust you are and to dust you will return" (Genesis 3:19). The curse of sin includes both spiritual and physical death. When my brother died, the process of returning to dust began.

We know from science that parents pass on their physical DNA to their offspring. The Bible teaches that human parents also pass along their spiritual condition to their offspring. It's funny how we have no problem understanding the concept of inheriting *physical* characteristics, but we balk at the concept of inheriting a broken *spiritual* relationship. And we balk at the concept that today we have inherited the curse that resulted from the sin committed by Adam and Eve that caused a broken relationship with God. Such consequences don't appear loving.

People enjoy talking about God's amazing and perfect love. Yes, God loves us, but His love can't excuse sin, because God is also *holy*. We are less apt to talk about that. God's holiness couldn't just overlook Adam or Eve's offense, and God's holiness can't "fix it" by giving their offspring (you and me) a clean slate.

In God, both love and holiness are in simultaneous and full operation all the time. Love and holiness exist together as one. There is no toggling back and forth between the two. It's like wearing a pair of glasses. We have to look through both lenses simultaneously in order for the glasses to provide us with perfect vision. In the same way, if we want to see God properly and perfectly, we have to put on "glasses" to view Him. One lens is love and the other lens is holiness. *Both* have to be simultaneously in front of our eyes in order to see God with clarity.

To be holy is to be clean, perfect, pure, and without blemish. The garden of Eden was based on a perfect plan without blemish because God Himself is perfect. For our protection, God banished

Adam and Eve and their descendants—us—from the garden. I propose, however, humanity was and is worthy to be banned anyway.

David Platt, author of *Radical*, explains, "It is not how small or large we would measure sin. What is significant is the greatness of the One who is sinned against. You sin against a rock, you're not very guilty. You sin against a man, you are guilty. You sin against an infinitely holy God and you are infinitely guilty and deserving of infinite destruction."[3] If you can't grasp that yet, you haven't recognized just how holy God is. Make Him cleaner, purer, and more perfect than you see Him now. Make God so holy that to leave His perfect plan is such an affront it is worthy of eternal consequences.

Did you ever clean a window, only to return later to find it still marred with streaks, smudges, and dirt? The imperfections were there when you first left; you just couldn't see them until the sun's position changed and revealed the truth about your original cleaning efforts. In the same way the sun shines new light on the true condition of our windows, God's holiness shines new light on the true condition of our hearts. We may look clean to others around us, but when we see "holy," our filth is revealed.

When the prophet Isaiah describes his vision of God, he writes, "I saw the Lord seated on a throne, high and exalted, and the train of his robe filled the temple" (Isaiah 6:1). He describes seraphs surrounding the throne and calling to one another: "Holy, holy, holy is the Lord Almighty; the whole earth is full of His glory" (Isaiah 6:2–3).

What did Isaiah do in the presence of "holy"? "Woe to me!" he cried. "I am ruined! For I am a man of unclean lips, and I live among a people of unclean lips, and my eyes have seen the King, the Lord Almighty" (Isaiah 6:5). The moment we are faced with the perfection of God, we see our imperfections. We see that "all our righteous acts are like filthy rags" (Isaiah 64:6). We see our sin.

Sin isn't a list of actions we deem unacceptable. Sin is an archery term that means to "miss the mark" or to miss the bulls-eye—to miss perfection.[4] Sin is anything that isn't perfect. Joni Eareckson Tada writes, "God is holy—that means he hates sin. God is just—that means he must punish sin. That should give us the shivers. We humans have no idea how offensive our sin is against a holy God."[5]

Perhaps you are tempted to think you don't want a holy God after all. But I want a holy God. I suspect, given time to think about it, you will too. I want a God who *never* makes a mistake. Don't you? I want a God who has *no imperfection* in His thinking or in any of His dealings with me. I want God to deal *perfectly* with the men who rape our daughters, the thieves who steal our belongings and drain our savings, and the people who murder.

But what if I am one of the criminals just mentioned, and I come to my senses? Or what if I am a law-abiding, good citizen who suddenly sees herself in front of God's holiness and sees filth? Then I would want love, the other lens through which I am seen. I would want forgiveness and a chance to change. In God, we have both—holiness and love. In the words of David Platt, "[God] absolutely *hates* sin and sinners, and He absolutely *loves* sinners. In the cross we see the absolute full expression of His holy wrath and His holy love coming together in one glorious moment for our salvation."[6]

In the garden of Eden, the curse on all mankind began because God is *holy*. In Jesus, we have payment for every sin because God is *love*. I believe when the pendulum of focus between holy and love swings to one side or the other instead of remaining perfectly balanced in the middle, confusion occurs. For example, if someone is told *only* about God's holiness, God may be seen as a dictator and unapproachable. If someone is told *only* about God's love and "asks Jesus into their heart" on the basis of love *alone*—in the absence of holiness—the individual may not even know why they needed Christ in the first place. I wonder if there are people who think they are Christians, but because they never grappled with the concept of God's holiness, they never saw their sin and understood their need for a Savior. And that may be our fault, the Christians who only told them half of the story.

> Faith is not a pathetic sentiment, but robust vigorous confidence built on the fact that God is holy love. You cannot see Him just now, you cannot understand what He is doing, but you know Him. Shipwreck occurs where there is not that mental poise which comes from being established on the eternal truth that God is holy love.[7]

Why did the curse happen to all people? God is holy, so He can't ignore sin. Our broken spiritual condition is passed to us along with our physical DNA. God is also love, so He makes a way for us to have an intimate relationship with Him again through Jesus.

Why did Jesus have to die?

Because of our inability

When we read the account of Adam and Eve eating from the tree of the knowledge of good and evil, we see something happening *internally* to them. They go from walking in the cool of the day with God in unhindered relationship to a state of being self-conscious, hiding in fear, and blaming others for their behavior (Genesis 3:7–8, 10, 12–13). Their *nature* changed the moment they broke away from the perfect plan for living created by a holy God.

Folks, the *types* of sins we commit are not so much the focus. The focus is the *nature* from which all sin springs—our "independent-go-against-God-I-want-to-do-it-my-way" nature. We are all in need of a Savior because each of us possesses an equally depraved nature. "The heart is deceitful above all things and beyond cure. Who can understand it?" (Jeremiah 17:9). There was a time when I did not believe that verse applied to my heart. After all, I thought I was good compared to others around me. When I finally let God's holiness shine a light on my heart, however, I saw things. Like the prideful thoughts I had when I did good things. Like the awful thoughts I had about people. It is stunning how ugly my heart can be.. We can all be tricked into thinking we are good people, and the reason for the deception is often "a mixture of cowardice and the protection of a civilized life."[8]

Currently, I live in a civil environment. Most people in my town are weathering the rough economic times and remain employed. As a community, we enjoy a level of wealth that keeps us comfortable. This civilized environment can trick me into thinking that I too am civilized. I rarely get angry, not because I am good, but because my environment cooperates with me on so many levels. As of today, my car starts when I turn the key. My home is well-maintained. I can communicate with virtually anyone I know on a whim or gather information from any corner of the world using my hand-held gadgets. My bills get paid because I currently have a job. My children are clothed and go to good public schools. My students are amazing people. What is there to get angry about?

See what I mean? Change my circumstances, or yours, and suddenly the truth about the sinful nature we inherited is exposed. What kind of nature rises up inside of us when people are difficult, our family is harmed, our bodies become sick, our checkbooks dry up, and our safety is threatened? That is the sinful nature. It is lurking in us all the while, but can be lured into slumber when unchallenged by our environment.

Not only can civility trick us into thinking we are better than others because we behave better; *fear* can trick us too. We can hide our sinful nature from the world around us because we are afraid of consequences such as what people will think of us, how the law will punish us, or what God will think. We can appear good and capable on the outside, but on the inside, we might be cowering in fear.

We need a Savior because we are stuck in our sinful nature. The holy God who created us cannot overlook our offenses. Thankfully, our holy God is also love, so He sent Jesus as a Savior.

Because of His ability

I have often listened to women express their confusion about the question of why Jesus had to die. They are concerned about how God could possibly sacrifice His Son. This is difficult to swallow since these women would never consider "sacrificing" one of their children for someone else. Now let's talk about why our Savior had to die for us.

God was not up in the sky above the garden of Eden thinking, *Hmmmm. What is the appropriate consequence for that action? Let me think. Death. I pick death.* Rather, when Adam and Eve broke away from God—Who *is* life—spiritual "death" occurred as an automatic and immediate natural *consequence.* Life or death, there was never an in-between. We then, as offspring of Adam and Eve, inherit this curse of death. The natural consequence of being disconnected from life was passed on to us through them. We are born into this condition—entrapped—and the only way out is through Jesus Christ. The Apostle Paul writes, "For as in Adam all die, so in Christ all are made alive" (1 Corinthians 15:22).

When our daughter was young, she was gripped by a fear of roller-coasters. Our family could never ride roller-coasters together. One parent would ride with one child, and the other parent would stay on the ground with our fearful child to watch and wait for the ride to be over. Then one amazing day, she faced her fear, made it through a long line without turning back, climbed into a snug roller-coaster cart, kept the lap bar down, and let the ride take her where it wished. She has since become a roller-coaster maniac.

Fear can only be conquered when a person faces the fear head-on and wins over that fear. It's the same with a curse. A curse cannot be broken unless someone faces it and beats it. In the case of the curse of death faced by Adam and his descendants, Someone actually needed to die and exchange death for life in order for the curse of death to be broken. Jesus could not crush the power of death by writing a mandate from a heavenly desk. He had to face death on our behalf and conquer it, which He most certainly did when He rose from the dead! Because Jesus broke the power of death, we now have assurance that indeed at the end of earth's history "'There will be no more death . . ." (Revelation 21:4) and "No longer will there be any curse . . ." (Revelation 22:3).

God couldn't have died for our sins because God can't die, since He is life. No *man* could have died for our sins because no man could have become a perfect sacrifice by living a sinless life. Only *Jesus*—because He was God in bodily form—could have faced death head on. And only Jesus could have operated in conjunction with God the Father and God the Holy Spirit to rise from the dead in resounding victory. By beating death, Jesus broke the curse of death.

God sacrificed His Son because
Jesus Christ was truly the only Man for the job.

Because Jesus was 100 percent God, He could get through this life without sin and present Himself as a perfect sacrifice. Because He was also 100 percent man, He could actually die. And then again, because he was 100 percent God, He could rise again.

In review, it is in the death of Jesus that we see the holiness and love of God working together simultaneously. Because God is holy, He couldn't have a relationship with us because of our sinful nature. Sin had to be paid for. Because God is love, God sent His Son, Jesus, to pay the penalty for our sins.

Why did Jesus have to die? Three reasons: We need a Savior. He had to break the curse of death. He was the only Person qualified for the job.

Why did God give us choice?

I have heard people ask many questions over the years regarding the introduction of sin into our lives. These include: Why did God set it up this way? Why did He give Adam and Eve a choice in the first place? Would the curse have occurred if Adam and Eve had not been given the one rule forbidding them to eat from the tree of the knowledge of good and evil? Would the curse have occurred if Satan had not been given a free will that allowed him to rebel against God? Why was this the plan, and how was that plan perfect?

We have been focusing on God's holiness quite a bit. Now let's reflect on love. I believe God created a world with choice because *without choice, love cannot exist.* If we want a world with love, we must have choice.

In the movie *Fireproof* (2008), a couple's marriage is on the brink of disintegration. The husband sets out to love his wife by doing a specific good thing for her every day. Each day, he is faithful to this task, but day after day goes by with no evidence that his good deeds are melting his wife's heart.

During this difficult time, two story lines simultaneously start to develop. The wife begins a friendship with a married man at work while her mother becomes ill and needs an expensive hospital bed and wheelchair. Stress mounts in the marriage until one day *the wife asks for a divorce.*

Despite this crushing setback, the husband remains undeterred in loving his wife well. He drains a hard-earned savings account he had set aside for a dream boat, and anonymously buys the hospital bed for his wife's mother.

The entire movie turns . . . and the marriage is saved . . . when the wife puts two and two together. She figures out that the husband had drained his coveted savings and purchased the hospital bed the day *after* she had asked for a divorce! Who would do that?

That's the whole point. He *chose* to drain his savings the day *after* she had asked for a divorce. Jesus tells us: "Greater love has no man than this, than to lay down his life for a friend" (John 15:13). This is what the husband did. He *chose* to lay down his life (savings) for a friend (his wife). Without *choice*, it is impossible to *love*. The wife melted in the face of such incredible, makes-no-sense-whatsoever kind of love, just like we all would. Without choice, we can't love like that.

I recently had the chance to prove my love for my husband in a similar way. I had been saving money since our oldest children were four. It was always the kids' nest egg. I dreamed of the day I would surprise them at high school graduation or on their wedding day with money toward a car or home.

Well, my husband started his own business about four years ago, and we needed to begin drawing on my savings account.

After a series of small withdrawals, we needed a large amount... The rest of my savings, in fact. Everything. I went to the bank and came home with all of my savings gone and a large check to place on my husband's desk.

Strangely, instead of being resentful, I found myself thinking about love and choice. I found myself walking around the house the next day grateful for the opportunity to *prove* to John that I loved him; yes, even that much, even enough to surrender my entire savings account. I can have a heart that is *willing* to give my husband all I have, but I cannot prove the *extent* of that love without opportunity.

If life had been created without choice, Adam and Eve would not have been able to stray from God's perfect plan for their existence. True. But hearts programmed to love can't really love. By God's choice, Adam and Eve began a life where love could freely flourish between Him and them. Yes, they eventually made the wrong choice. But then again, God *chose* to push through His holiness and hatred of impurity. He paid for all the impurity of history with His Son's death on the cross. That's how we *know* God loves us. We think we want God to remove our ability to choose hatred, but in doing so, we would relinquish our ability to choose love.

Why did God give us choice? Without choice, love cannot exist.

Who is Satan?

The first verse of the Bible is, "In the beginning God created the heavens and the earth" (Genesis 1:1). The heavens not only included stars and planets, but angels as well. Angels were present when the earth was created.

> Where were you when I laid the earth's foundation? . . . Who marked off its dimensions? . . . On what were its footings set or who laid its cornerstone—while the morning stars sang together and all the angels shouted for joy?
>
> —Job 38:4–7[9]

A revolt occurred among the angels. You can read about this revolt in Ezekiel 28:11–19 and Isaiah 14:12–14. Satan was originally the most beautiful and greatest of the angels God created (Ezekiel 28:12),[10] and was one of God's cherubim—the order of angels created to guard the holiness of God (Genesis 3:22–24, Ezekiel 28:14).[11] Being the highest of all angelic creatures, the devil was the only created being that had nothing more beautiful between himself and God. He became prideful and wanted to be worshipped as God (Isaiah 14:12–14).[12] God cast Satan from heaven, and one-third of the other angels chose to leave with him (Revelation 12:4).[13] The fallen angels that left with Satan are known as demons. Together, the devil and demons are referred to as the "enemy" in Scripture. Meanwhile, there remains a host of angels who did not participate in the revolt (Daniel 7:10). These are about the business of worshipping God (Isaiah 6:1–3), carrying out God's work (Luke 1:26–33, Luke 2:8–15), and ministering to God's children (Hebrews 1:14).

Jesus was in heaven and watched Satan being cast down. Luke records Jesus as saying, "I saw Satan fall like lightning from heaven" (Luke 10:18). Because of Satan's plummet, there is now an organized spiritual world attempting to thwart God's story on earth.

News about the presence of an enemy can be very discouraging if we don't understand the dot from a new angle. So far, we have discussed the dot as a representation of our life spans. Let's take it further now. All of Satan's operative powers are also safely contained in the dot on the string of eternity. His ability to interfere began when he was cast out of heaven to earth (Ezekiel 28:16–17), and it will end when he is cast into his own hell forever (Revelation 20:10). Satan's time isn't only short; it's *very* short.

We don't need to be afraid of Satan's involvement in history, because the victory in the larger story God is telling is already won, as we have established. But we need to be aware of the battle. We are surrounded on all sides by the world—over which Satan has influence—and by Satan and his demons.

Not only does Satan have a dot-sized speck of time in which to operate, he also has limited power within that time frame. Since he is a created being, he is not all-knowing, or all-powerful, or present everywhere like God is. Also, he operates within boundaries set by Jesus (Mark 1:34) and boundaries set by God (Job 1:12, 2:6). And he can be resisted (James 4:7).

So, though the devil is active, he still falls under the authority of God. In the book of Job, Job is characterized as "blameless and upright . . . the greatest man among all the people of the East" (Job 1:1, 3). The devil tells God that the only reason Job is a good man is because God had been exceptionally good to him. To prove Satan wrong, God grants him permission to test Job, but with strict boundaries. In Job 1:12 we read, "The Lord said to Satan, 'Very well, then, everything he has is in your hands, but on the man himself do not lay a finger.'" Those of you who are familiar with the entire story know that Satan goes back a second time to request permission to try Job. His request is granted, but once more with boundaries that Job's life be spared (Job 2:6).

I am comforted by the fact that the devil has to consult God before touching me, and then, has to honor the boundaries God has established. I am also comforted by the fact that the only suffering allowed through God's fingers is for my good. At the end of the book of Job, we read that after much anguish, Job has some sort of "aha" moment, and says to God, "My ears had heard of you but now my eyes have seen you. Therefore, I despise myself and repent in dust and ashes" (Job 42:5–6). We aren't given any more details, but what is clear is that this exceedingly righteous and blameless man sees God more vividly than he had before. Whatever growth occurred enabled Job to see additional sin in his heart and repent, after which "the Lord made him prosperous again and gave him twice as much as he had before" (Job 42:10).

The battle Satan wages against God is limited and never "out of control." As in Job's case, whatever interference God permits Satan to create in our lives is for our good. In addition, in Christ we can limit Satan's ability to mess with us. You see, the reason the devil has any power at all is because he will wriggle into any room *we* give him. Knowing his strategies of deceit can only make us better equipped to live in victory instead of defeat. This "spiritual battle" is discussed later in this book in Chapter Eight: As a Soldier. Somehow, I missed being exposed to the realities of evil in the world, or I failed to comprehend what I was taught. This left me naïve, ill-informed, and ill-equipped to deal with traumatic events that would follow.

It wasn't until a few years before I started writing this book that I began to understand, Satan is a murderer and a liar (John 8:44) and an accuser (Revelation 12:10). He is our adversary (1 Peter 5:8). He masquerades as an angel of light (2 Corinthians 11:14), and seeks opportunities to attack us (Luke 4:13). Later in the book, I will outline the opportunities Satan saw to derail me as a Christ follower. He saw his chance, threw me lies, and I foolishly believed.

The "enemy" is alive and well today. He wants to keep people from hearing about Jesus at all. Once someone does come to terms with the life-saving assurance of knowing God through Jesus, the devil then aims to derail, ruin, and render each follower of Christ helpless and unfruitful. You do not have to be derailed.

Who is the devil? A fallen angel with limited and temporary power.

Why is Satan permitted to operate today?

Recall how everything constrained by a time frame is represented by a dot, including the time Satan is permitted to directly interfere with our lives. At one point, the devil made a *futile* attempt to convince Jesus to trade in His control of the string (the eternal story) for a dot (the finite length of time Satan operates on earth). Just before Jesus began His public ministry, He was tempted in the wilderness. After fasting for forty days and forty nights, the devil tempted Jesus three times (Matthew 4:1–11). One of those temptations included Satan offering Him the world.

> Again, the devil took him to a very high mountain and showed him all the kingdoms of the world and their splendor. "All this I give you," he said, "if you will bow down and worship me." Jesus said to him, "Away from me Satan! For it is written: 'Worship the Lord your God, and serve him only.'" Then the devil left him, and angels came and attended to him.
>
> —Matthew 4:8–11

Make no mistake—no part of God's story was threatened when Jesus was tested. Being 100 percent God, Jesus could not—and cannot—sin. The New Testament also teaches Jesus has all power and authority (Matthew 28:18, Colossians 1:16), including over the world. The devil was able to offer Jesus the world because he was "the prince of this world" (John 12:31, 14:30, 16:11). He still is today. Jesus states clearly, however, when referring to Satan, "He has no hold on me" (John 14:30). The devil wanted to extend his miniscule length of influence, but alas, Jesus was and is immovable in his commitment to guard eternity. So for now—for a tiny span of time—the devil operates. Meanwhile, God is doing something spectacular with this chaotic dot of time.

On certain days, when I watch the news, I have to admit the thought crosses my mind, *Lord, how can Your holiness bear to look at this one more day? Why don't You just end it all?* Then I imagine God's response: "Because, Laurie, I am waiting one more day for more people to come to know Me—to accept My gift of love for their sin, so that I can give them a perfect eternity."

I have been influenced by Joni Eareckson Tada's reflections on 2 Peter 3:9: "The Lord is not slow in keeping his promise, as some understand slowness. He is patient with you, not wanting anyone to perish, but everyone to come to repentance." The sun came up today because a holy God is bearing with all the wrongs of the world for *one more day* in order that everyone in the world can have another opportunity to learn about Jesus. Joni says, "He is holding off . . . so that, heaven willing, my neighbor, my relatives, and the people who work in my community will come to repentance."[14]

Some might envision there is a giant tussle in the sky whereby God and Satan are wrestling over the fate of souls. They imagine that sometimes God is winning and sometimes Satan is winning, but they believe in the end God will overcome. This is an inaccurate perception. There is no tussle between God and Satan. As discussed already, Satan operates within boundaries established by God. Rather, angels and demons are fighting against each other, and we are the prize they're fighting for![15] God is winning every minute. God is *waiting*, not losing. Big difference.

One day, the curtain will come down, the devil will be thrown into his own pit of hell forever (Matthew 25:41, Revelation 20:10), all causes of sad tears will be removed from the earth (Revelation 21:4), and the entire earth will be restored (Revelation 21:1, 5). Heaven on earth will be a reality forever for all people who accept the payment Jesus Christ made for their sins—a Son sent from a *holy* God who *loved* them beyond measure.

If the curtain were to come down today, the hatred and chaos in the world would end. What a relief. But other things would end as well, like the opportunity for everyone I know to have an opportunity to experience God's holy love through Jesus Christ. So you know what? I can wait another day—a miniscule amount of time in light of the string—and I can let God decide the perfect time for His return.

Until then, you and I live under the curse.

Why is the devil allowed to operate right now? So he doesn't operate in our eternity (the string). His activities stay contained in a dot. God has allowed Satan's brief reign to continue so everyone on earth who does not yet know Christ will have another opportunity to receive Him and to have eternal life.

How is God in control of this chaos?

In order to answer this question, several understandings are needed. First, the story God is telling with history is undeterred by chaos; we cannot stop it. Second, chaos is sifted through God's fingers. The chaos that comes our way is for our ultimate good. Third, our response to chaos dictates whether or not we experience the good God intends for us to experience. These three understandings allow us the benefit of resting in God's control over history as well as His control over the chaos in our lives.

Understanding #1: History is undeterred by chaos

From the moment evil entered the world's story, God has been pursuing all people. Right after Adam and Eve hid from God in Eden; He walked in the garden of Eden in the cool of the evening and called out, "Where are you?" (Genesis 3:9). *Please circle that in your Bible.* It's a key part of God's story. Those words mark the beginning of God's pursuit to get the garden back. God intends to gain it *all* back when this chapter of history ends, and He establishes the new heaven and new earth. One of the wonderful things He will get back is an unhindered relationship with each person living eternally with Him. The new earth will be full of people living happily ever after in perfect harmony with God and with each other.

Through the ages, God has remained accessible to us. In Acts 17:27–28, we learn, ". . . he is not far from each one of us. For in him we live and move and have our being." God did not distance Himself from us; rather, we distanced ourselves from Him. I liken the process of reconciliation we see unfolding in scripture to that of a parent trying to restore a broken relationship with a disgruntled son or daughter. Often, we must approach the offended child in stages in order to woo him or her back. We first knock gently on a bedroom door hoping for a response. Once we receive a gruff invitation, we enter gingerly. Then slowly, but surely, we press in closer as the child begins to respond to our love once again.

In the Bible, we can see God's purposeful intent, in ways similar to that of a parent, to repair our broken relationship with Him. Since God uttered the question, "Where are you?" He has demonstrated relentless interest in remaining close to His people. In Exodus, we read that God traveled in front of the Israelites as a cloud by day and a pillar of fire by night (Exodus 13:21–22). Then God *pressed in closer*. He determined to no longer travel in front of them. God instructed the people of Israel to erect a tabernacle—a large worship tent—so He could dwell *with* His people (Exodus 25:8; 2 Samuel 7:6). Then, God *pressed in even closer* when Jesus came to live among us on earth as is described by the apostle John: "The Word became flesh and made his dwelling among us" (John 1:14).

Now we arrive at today, the time in history in which you and I live. After Jesus died and rose again, God was able to press in closer yet again by actually coming to dwell inside each follower of Jesus through the indwelling of His Holy Spirit (Romans 8:9, Titus 3:4–7).

I hope you are beginning to see God's initiative to restore His relationship with humanity by consistently *pressing in closer*. He will press in even closer at the end of time when we will once again enjoy an intimate relationship with Him as seen throughout Revelation 21 and 22:

> Then I saw a new heaven and a new earth, for the first heaven and the first earth had passed away . . . I saw the Holy City, the new Jerusalem, coming down out of heaven from God, prepared as a bride for her husband. And I heard a loud voice from the throne saying, "Now the dwelling of God is with men, and he will live with them. They will be his people, and God himself will be with them and be their God. He will wipe every tear from their eyes . . ."
>
> —Revelation 21:1–4

Notice that the imagery used by the Apostle John to describe God's intimacy with His children is that of the love of a husband for his bride. John continues to convey a vision of the open access God's people will have with Him: "The city does not need the sun or moon to shine on it, for the glory of God gives it light, and the Lamb is its lamp. The nations will walk by its light . . . On no day will its gates be shut . . ." (Revelation 21:23–25) and "No longer will there be any curse . . . They will see his face . . ." (Revelation 22:3–4).

Through all of the centuries, through all the wars and earthquakes and hurricanes and wrongs, the sun has come up every morning, and God's plan of relentless pursuit of people has never been deterred. That same plan is still unfolding above our heads today, and nothing can stop it.

I hope you see the love of God pushing through His holiness to offer us payment for sin through Jesus Christ. He does this so that at the end of history, when heaven comes to earth for the rest of eternity, God in a sense can get the garden of Eden back. Instead of a garden inhabited by just Adam and Eve, with whom God enjoyed a personal relationship for a limited time, the entire earth will be inhabited by individuals from every nation, tribe, people, and language (Revelation 7:9) with whom God will enjoy an intimate relationship forever. The garden of Eden had a river of water (Genesis 2:10–14), but on the new earth there will be the "river of the water of life, as clear as crystal, flowing from the throne of God and of the Lamb" (Revelation 22:1). One of the most exciting correlations to the state we will experience in the garden is evident in the Apostle John's words in Revelation 22:3: "No longer will there be any curse." There was no curse at the beginning of the garden of Eden, and there will be no curse at the end of time.

How is God in control of the chaos of history? Have you noticed it yet? In all the years since time began, absolutely *nothing* has stopped this larger, grander, absolutely magnificent story from unfurling above our heads. History is safe. God's unstoppable story reigns above all of us (Psalm 103:19).

Not only is the grand scale of history safely in God's hands, so is your personal life's story. If you are not a Christian yet, know that God has been in relentless pursuit of you since the moment you were born. You are one of the reasons why He allowed the sun to come up again today! (Even reading this book is part of His pursuit.) If you are a Christian and have just learned the term really means to be a Christ follower, but you are not yet, then hear the garden echoes of His fervent pursuit through the ages. Bend your ear and listen to Him calling, "Where are you?"

Understanding #2: Chaos is sifted through God's fingers

This chaotic world throws trouble at us from every direction. We complicate life for ourselves when we make unwise decisions and suffer the consequences. Trouble is also caused by people around us who make decisions that result in grief and pain. We live in a world that bombards us with unworthy, unpleasant, and dishonorable things. Chaos surrounds us.

How is God in charge of all this mess with regard to you and me? This question is answered with the second understanding: Chaos is sifted through His fingers for our ultimate good. We learned that God was a "yes" God in the garden of Eden (see "Why is God not to blame for Dan's death?"). He still is a "yes" God; He loves to say yes to us! Even earthly fathers who have sinful natures know how to give good gifts to their children. God is perfect, so logic dictates that we can trust Him to be generous in the same way we expect good earthly fathers to be generous.

> Which of you, if his son asks for bread, will give him a stone? Or if he asks for a fish, will give

> him a snake? If you, then, though you are evil, know how to give good gifts to your children, how much more will your Father in heaven give good gifts to those who ask him!
>
> —Matthew 7:9–11

Based on this line of thinking, when I pray protection over my family, I believe God longs to say "yes." When I ask for my daughter to reap the reward of earning a place in a top high school band because of her hard work as a flutist, I believe God longs to say "yes." When I ask God to heal someone who is sick or provide a job for someone unemployed, He longs to say "yes." I can rest in God's desire to say "yes," which is why I can trust when God says "no."

"And we know that in all things God works for the good of those who love him, who have been called according to his purpose" (Romans 8:28). This verse isn't for everyone. Did you catch the condition for the promise? It's for people who love Him and are called according to His good purposes.

God serves as a protective filter over the circumstances of Christians who love Him, and causes all things to work for good. When God says "no," it is for our good. Because He longs to say "yes," I do not believe He says "no" matter of factly because He knows the eventual good produced by our suffering. I believe He is tender in His response when the answer to our pleadings is "no" to that job offer, "no" to a dream we have for our child, and "no" to desired test results at the doctor's office. I imagine God saying very gently, "I would love to grant your request, but if you can trust Me, I have an even better plan than what you had in mind. If you can trust Me, I will do amazing things through the suffering caused by today's circumstances. I have something better in mind because I can see the eternal picture; otherwise, I would say 'yes.'" If I am ever in an auto accident, for example, I know it's not something God has done to me, but that He has *allowed* chaos to sift through His fingers for my good.

Our Father not only loves us, He is also perfect. He never makes a mistake with us. God is working all things for good through a precise and perfect combination of "yes" and "no" answers. The cursed world comes at us from all sides, but God protects us by allowing only what produces good. This is what it means to live ABOVE the chaos. The result is *always* good for those who love Him and are called according to His good purposes.

I am reminded of crucifixion day when it *didn't* look good. It didn't look like a story of victory. All of the players in this historic event were weak. Pontius Pilate feared the people, and handed his decision-making authority to an angry crowd (Matthew 27:24), and the high priest accused Jesus of blasphemy (Matthew 26: 65), and the religious leaders said He was worthy of death (Matthew 26:66). This is an extreme example of a person's life being twisted and turned by the sins of other people. They were spinning Christ's life that day into what appeared to be a chaotic mess. It looked like God had lost control.

Today, we know the incompetent leaders involved with Christ's crucifixion were all part of the beautiful plan to have our sins forgiven. Joni Eareckson Tada conveys her understanding of God's constant control over all world events this way: "He steers the sin already in peoples' hearts so that sinners unwittingly fulfill God's plans and not merely their own."[16] God was doing the steering on crucifixion day.

One of the events leading to Christ's crucifixion was Judas Iscariot's betrayal of Jesus. The devil had previously prompted Judas to betray Jesus (John 13:2). At the famous "last supper" with

His disciples, Jesus had given bread to Judas. The Apostle John tells us: "As soon as Judas took the bread, Satan entered into him" (John 13:27). Judas then left Jesus and the disciples. He later led soldiers and religious officials to an olive grove where Jesus was gathered with His disciples (John 18:2–3). Satan himself was involved in the events on crucifixion day but never for a moment did he have the upper hand. The cross was a perfect victory intended for the benefit of all of us. That gruesome death beat the curse of death (see "Why did Jesus have to die?"), and became a perfect payment for our sins; thus, we were given the option of living eternally in the presence of God.

In his book, *Prayer: Does It Make Any Difference?*, Philip Yancey quotes the great German preacher Helmut Thielicke, who suffered greatly for opposing Hitler:

> …if I had ever dreamed that God was only carrying out his design and plan through all these woes, that in the midst of my cares and troubles and despair his harvest was ripening, and that everything was pressing on toward his last kingly day—if I had known this I would have been more calm and confident; yes, then I would have been more cheerful and far more tranquil and composed.[17]

Last year, I met a woman who experienced a rough childhood of severe abuse. God did not do that. People with sinful natures and sinful choices did that. The curse did that. This woman became a Christian and lives today as a foster parent and mother of both adopted and natural children. She irrevocably states that her passion is a direct result of being rescued from her abusive past. The childhood trauma has lost its debilitating sting. As Beth Moore states, "You cannot amputate your history from your destiny, because that is redemption."[18]

Understanding #3: Our response to chaos is critical

Thus far in our discussion of how it is that God is in control of chaos, we have established that the story God is telling is undeterred by chaos and that chaos is sifted through God's fingers. The final component of understanding how God is in control involves our response to chaos. Nothing and no one can ever stop God's larger story in history, but at a personal level, our response to chaos plays a crucial role in whether the struggles are used for good in our lives or are used to damage us further. About thirty years ago, I memorized the following verse in a version of the Bible that was popular at the time, the *New American Standard.* I still prefer this translation for this verse above all other translations because of one three-letter word.

> Consider it all joy, my brethren, when you encounter various trials, knowing that the testing of your faith produces endurance. And *let* endurance have its perfect result, that you may be perfect and complete, lacking in nothing.
>
> —James 1:2–4, emphasis mine

Go ahead and circle the word *let.* When the trials come, we either *let* endurance have its perfect result, or we respond in some other way. These responses may include complaining, working harder, stressing, withdrawing, or taking a break from the "good fight" for a season and doing life our own way for a while. Jesus *let* crucifixion happen, and the foster mom described above has *let* abuse become a redeemable part of her past.

When Dan died, I did not *let* endurance have its perfect result. I left to do life my own way for a while. Yes, I was in pain, but because I did not *let,* all I had to show for those seven years when it was over was a mess to clean up. Since then, I have had other opportunities to *let* endurance have its perfect result.

In 1997, I was deeply wounded by someone very close to me. The offense was so great that my world crumbled. I was empty, swirling, confused, and desperate. Instead of leaving to do life my own way like I had done when Dan died, I *let*. I called professionals who could teach me how to cope and was introduced to *Freedom in Christ Ministries*. I learned to recognize lies and to replace them with truths. This practice brought about transformation in my life.

I selected trustworthy friends to pray for me and be at my beck and call for counsel 24/7, and I became involved in a Bible study called *A Woman's Heart: God's Dwelling Place* written by Beth Moore.[19] The study kept me turning the pages of my Bible every day because I had homework to complete. Through daily doses of God's Word, I was transformed some more.

I am seventeen years beyond that traumatic time. I cannot begin to explain how different I am because of that suffering. God gave me so much of Himself and changed me so radically that I believe nearly everything I do and think today is still rooted in what God did in me through that sad event. God used the suffering to make me more perfect and complete. I wouldn't want to suffer that way again, *but I gained so much through it that it's okay the circumstances occurred.*

What I have learned I passed along to my daughter who was diagnosed with lupus in her junior year of high school. When she left for college, the disease activity was much improved, but not yet completely under control. Labs came back early in her freshman year indicating she was having a flare-up severe enough to try a new medication. One night, as we spoke on the phone, she understandably asked, "Why is God doing this?"

I responded by reminding her God isn't doing this. I told her that it is death, sickness, our own sinful natures, and the sinful natures of people around us that hurt us. This is all part of the curse. God will win over that, I explained, by using the suffering for her good—if she *lets* Him.

"How can this be used for good, Mom?"

"Well, you will actually *experience* God's peace in hard circumstances instead of just hearing that it is possible. You can draw closer to God, and learn even more about His love in ways not possible without the suffering. Friends who observe your life and your faith-filled response will learn about Jesus, and some may come to know Him. You may learn to comprehend some things better than your friends, like the brevity of life, or that when things go well, it's the grace of God not your self-effort. The list goes on—if you *let* Him."

As I traverse these confusing and disconcerting medical waters with my amazing daughter, I find great comfort in trusting the higher story unfolding above her head and mine. God would not have let the tough stuff sift through His fingers, so to speak, if it wasn't going to be for our good. That's the twist. Satan will try to destroy. People will commit offenses against us on purpose and by accident. Imperfect DNA may tumble together inside our children. But in spite of these, and no matter what, if we walk closely with God and *let*, He will turn all "harm" into so much good it will leave heads spinning, including our own.

This season of world history—between the times of the curse instituted in the garden of Eden and the end of time when heaven comes to rest on a restored earth—is not what God originally intended for us. It is tainted by the curse. But His story for history, and for each of us, still reigns supreme until the day evil is eradicated forever. The devil can do nothing to stop God's story within history, and the same can be true for you personally—if you *let* yourself connect with God's story instead of holding on to one of your own making.

I am now in the autumn years of my life and one *let* has led to another. I am learning to *let* God use suffering for good results—immeasurable, eternal, life-changing, and breathtaking results that can only be attributed to the work of God.

It's here I gain additional insight into what God is accomplishing on earth through Christians. Not only is He providing time for us to give everyone on earth an opportunity to hear about Christ, He is also using the chaos to grow us and increase our ability to display His strength and beauty to the world. God has chosen not to defeat Satan all by Himself. Instead, He is allowing us the privilege of participating in shining light in the darkness and then sharing the eternal victory in heaven—you and me—frail bodied and trapped in sin apart from Christ. But when filled with the Holy Spirit of God, we become a God-sized force. As Christ followers, we win. The entire plan is an affront to Satan.[20]

How is God in control of this chaos? First, God's larger story in history is undeterred by chaos. Second, chaos is sifted through His fingers for our ultimate good. Third, our response is critical. If we *let* God use the suffering for our good, we participate in God's victory by displaying His strength and beauty to the world.

What decision faces each of us?

Now that you are privy to the eternal grand plan that has been unfolding around each of us from the beginning of eternity, I hope that:

- You see how earth's story was launched in love.
- You see how safe you are in God's hands because He is in complete control of a plan headed towards a pure and incredible end. The

plan is available to you if you choose to embrace it, if you *let* Him control your life.

- You see that the entire plan hinges on the person of Jesus Christ.

Don't you want to pause and contend with the facts that have been presented about Jesus? Don't you want to make sure your life is connected to this incredible, eternal plan?

I got to thinking about the decision we must all make about Jesus when my husband's daughter, Elizabeth, was living with us while finishing college. She was busy taking courses full-time and working part-time. As if she didn't have enough going on, she was in the process of having her jaw and teeth misalignments repaired.

When John and I received the cost estimate for Elizabeth's oral care, one thing was certain: Elizabeth, our flat-broke college student, couldn't pay for it. I ran across the checkbook register a few weeks ago. The amount was over $6,000. We happened to have it at that time. So I drove to the orthodontic office and paid Elizabeth's bill in advance, and in full.

At that point, Elizabeth had a choice. She could accept our payment for her teeth or retract our money from the orthodontist and insist that she pay the bill instead. Imagine her marching right into that office and demanding that our money not count for her teeth! In such a case, she would then owe the astronomical amount herself, incurring a lot of suffering and heartache—and it would take "forever" to pay off. Elizabeth was prudent and let *our* payment count for *her* bill.

Elizabeth's decision reminds me of the one we must all make about the cross. Jesus paid each person's sin bill in full. Here are the choices you (and I) have to make: Are you going to march into God's "office" and demand that He return Christ's payment because you don't want it to count for your "sin bill"? Or would you rather simply tell Jesus, "Thank You. I will let Your payment count for me." Personally, I want you to accept what has already been paid. Please don't look at God and tell Him you want Him to take back His payment. I want you in heaven with me!

Every analogy breaks down at some point. While Elizabeth would have been foolish to reject the payment in full, she could have done so and scraped together cash little by little to pay the bill herself. This scenario is not possible with regard to salvation, which can never be earned (Ephesians 2:8–9) because God is holy (see "Why did 'the curse' happen to all people?"). Only when we see ourselves in light of His exquisite perfection can we understand it is impossible to acquire an intimate relationship with God's flawless purity on our own. Only when we see ourselves compared to His holiness can we understand that our sinful nature is worthy of the death penalty—*a bill Jesus paid for us in full because He loves us.* He paid it by dying and rising from the dead (Romans 4:25–5:2). He conquered death; something you and I can never do.

Jesus didn't come to earth and "sort of" do life as a human being. He didn't come down and just "take a look around." He came to *fully* participate in the human experience; yet, He was without sin. He came to *fully* commit Himself to being a perfect sacrifice. It is for this sacrifice that He came in human flesh. His death *fully* counted for the forgiveness of our sins, and it smashed the curse of death. We can *fully* trust Him for eternal life.

The famous words of John 3:16 state, "For God so *loved* the world that he *gave* his one and only Son that *whoever believes in* him shall not perish but have *eternal life.*" Put simply, a Christian is someone who is trusting in Jesus alone to forgive sins and to save him or her. He or she believes this is the only pathway to an eternal life, which begins now and continues in heaven. As we consider the decision that faces each of us, it is my hope that:

- You grapple with the concept of God's holiness and your sinfulness, and see your need for a Savior.
- You see a holy Jesus took your sin on the cross and made a way for you to go to heaven.
- You see God pursued you since the beginning of time, and He is calling your name.
- You understand God is telling a cohesive, dramatic, and unfolding story of His plan for eternity. He invites each individual on earth to join in—if he or she chooses.
- You realize becoming a Christian seems reasonable and not some blind, nonsensical leap of faith.
- You understand when Jesus said, "It is finished," He meant He alone finished the work of salvation and there was and is nothing more to be added.

Your salvation has never been about you doing anything. It's always been about God rescuing you from a debt you can't pay, just like our Elizabeth was rescued when she could not pay her orthodontic bill.

If you want to have your sins paid for, thank God for what He has done for you, and let His death count for your personal sin debt instead of trying to pay the debt yourself. Placing your faith in Christ's death *alone* for the forgiveness of your sins is what allows you to be adopted into the family of God. You can express your desire to experience Christ's forgiveness through prayer. A prayer does not make you a Christian, but it can solidify the decision in your memory. You get to choose. If you decide, "Yes," and want help expressing your decision to God, here's an idea of what to say to mark this momentous occasion.

Dear Jesus,

I see my sinful nature when I compare myself to Your holiness. I see my need for a Savior. Thank You for already paying my sin bill to God in full. I accept that payment for myself and trust in You alone for the forgiveness of my sins and for eternity in heaven. In addition, I give You my heart and my life. I want You to be in charge of both.

In Jesus' name, amen.

If through this prayer, you have expressed your commitment to trust Christ for the forgiveness of your sins and you have decided to follow Christ, then congratulations! You are now a child of God! You have been adopted into God's family through Christ's flesh-and-blood death on the cross.

Our youngest son is adopted. It was the most amazing experience to receive his birth certificate after the court appearance at which he became our child. The birth certificate listed John and me as the parents on the day of his birth. We were not present that day, but from a legal standpoint, adoption means someone is *treated as if he never belonged to anyone else.*

If you have already made a decision for Christ, I can't wait to meet you in heaven. You and I already have an eternal relationship even though we have never met. Thank Jesus today for the fact that you know Him already.

If you are not ready to place your faith in Christ today, at least now you know what that means. I urge you not to wait too long, however, because none of us knows when life on earth will end. In addition, life on earth is fuller, richer, better, and more fulfilling when we live:

- within God's fullest protection,
- in intimate relationship with Him,

- connected to His power and promises,
- and with the knowledge that our lives will count for more than a chaotic "dot" in time.

I want you to experience this eternal life. It begins now with an uninterrupted relationship with a loving and holy God, and it culminates with heaven.

"Today, if you hear his voice, do not harden your hearts" (Hebrews 4:7).

What decisions face each of us? Are we going to trust God with this brief dot of a life so we can participate in His eternal string? Are we going to trust Jesus *alone* for our salvation? Are we going to trust Jesus—the One who died for our sins and then rose again—to break the curse so we can live forever?

Why are we here?

> You are the light of the world. A city set on a hill cannot be hidden. Neither do people light a lamp and put it under a bowl. Instead they put it on its stand, and it gives light to everyone in the house. In the same way, let your light shine before men, that they may see your good deeds and praise your Father in heaven.
>
> —Matthew 5:14–16

There are a variety of good answers to the question, "Why are we here?" Some say worship is our purpose. Good answer. Some say prayer is to be our main business. Great. Some say Bible knowledge. Some say service. Good answers! All of these responses are fabulous—except for today. Today, I want to explore a particular train of thought that begins with the question: What's the one thing you *can't* do when you get to heaven?

In heaven, you can enjoy the presence of God and Jesus (Revelation 22:4), read the Bible (1 Peter 1:24–25), serve (Revelation 22:3), live in community (Revelation 21:23–24; 22:3), and lead (Revelation 21:24). What you *can't* do is invite anyone else to heaven. The curtain will have closed. The chances will be gone. The holiness of God will not bear one more day of "the cowardly, the unbelieving, the vile, the murderers, the sexually immoral, those who practice magic arts, the idolaters and all liars" (Revelation 21:8).

All Christians around the globe should be graciously inviting people to heaven; they should be showing them the way. As a cohesive unit on earth, we are to be as beautiful as a city of lights under a night sky. If this is the ideal, then why do I feel so alone sometimes? Why does it feel like I have to check around corners and look in the shadows to find Christians? Could it be we are hiding the light of Jesus under a bowl instead of living transparently for all to see?

The challenge to be a light in a dark world seems daunting. Thankfully, Jesus didn't leave us alone to do this huge work. He sent the Holy Spirit. "And I will ask the Father, and he will give you another Counselor to be with you forever—the Spirit of truth . . . But you know him, for he lives with you and will be in you" (John 14:16–17). Wow! God's Spirit lives inside of us, and if the Spirit is in control instead of us, we can shine Christ's character to the world!

Life under the curse makes the world a dark place, but even the smallest of lights shines brightly in darkness. Together, as Christians envelop the globe from each of our individual addresses and through each of our individual efforts, we can unite forces to become the light of the world we are called to be. I wish for God to look down upon the earth and see our planet as a giant sparkler because each of His children is living as a light on a stand instead of under a bowl. History is headed toward heaven on earth whether we act like a light or not. Remember the prior review of how God has been pressing in closer with each segment of history (see "How is God in control of this mess?")? God hasn't stopped His relentless pursuit of *all people.* We have the amazing opportunity to join His search party and participate in growing the number of people who are going to heaven. Remember, the sun came up today in order for God's *love* to give everyone one more chance to come to know Him before His *holiness* decides to bear sin no longer.

What does a light look like? *Being a light simply means you aren't hiding the fact that you are a Christian. You are living transparently. If an opportunity arises to bring up your spiritual life as readily as you do any other part of your life, then you do so.*

I remember a call my daughter made from her college campus one evening. During our conversation, I heard her say to a passerby, "I am going to Bible study!" In explaining the interruption to our conversation, she said, "Sorry, Mom, someone just asked where I was headed." That's what I mean by living transparently. My daughter didn't say, "Just across campus" or "Nowhere special" or "Briscoe" (the name of the building to which she was headed). I am guilty of providing answers such as these that are truthful, but hide my Christianity. Instead, my daughter spoke the transparent truth, "I am going to Bible study!" and in doing so, associated herself with the God of the Bible, or the title of Christian.

All of us should possess such candid and ready transparency. No hiding. My daughter just answers questions honestly. Her normal college-life conversations about studying, soccer, and relationships are sprinkled with words like pray, God, Jesus, and faith. It sometimes feels to her that no one is responding overtly to the spiritual side of her life, but people are watching. When one of her friends has a spiritual question, they come find her. They know she is a safe person to ask, and what follows can be a one or two-hour discussion about God and His Son, Jesus.

Every person in history who has trusted Christ as his or her personal Savior will be in heaven forever. Each of us has the job of allowing God to use us to introduce people to Jesus through our unique personalities, talents, gifts, and opportunities. If we each lived with such a purpose, it would be impossible for us to comprehend the far-reaching effects we would have on the world and on heaven.

This issue of being transparent about our faith threads through this book until addressed thoroughly in Chapter Twenty-One: Loving People Who Don't Yet Know Christ. For now, I am planting the seed that we don't need to bring up Jesus every time we speak to others, but at some point, we need to associate His name with our lives. And at some point, people need to hear specifically about Jesus. No one gets to heaven by knowing a nice person or seeing someone wearing a cross necklace. A person can only get to heaven if someone loves him or her enough to explain how to know Jesus.

Why do we sometimes share our struggles with a co-worker or neighbor, but leave out parts that would expose our faith—that we are praying or we are memorizing verses that encourage us in our times of crisis? I have omitted such details, have you? When we keep our faith a secret, we don't give any room for God to influence our relationships and woo people to Him. We must stop keeping our mouths closed. There will be a day when the sun does not come up anymore, because the Son will have returned to lift the curse. Until then, we need to increase the size of heaven and increase our amount of light by living authentically and openly! Let's not hide! Let's make this earth sparkle!

Why are we here? To be bright lights in a dark world.

Wrapping up the big questions

I had to dig down deep to discover the root cause of my pain in response to Dan's tragic accident. Were the answers I received to the ten questions comprehensive? No. Did I learn enough to settle my soul on these weighty matters? Absolutely. God allowed me to see the tragedy from the vantage point of His larger, cohesive story. He used the answers to lay a new groundwork for my faith and began to grow a desire in me for more understanding and continued healing. Just like the passengers on the airplane responded differently to the tired father once they learned he had recently become a widower, I hope this question and answer section has provided a context that allows you to see your difficulties differently—in ways that settle your soul like they did mine.

Chapter Four

Are You Living ABOVE the Chaos or IN It?

Well, it is time to ask the question: How are you doing with chaos? Are you able to lift your eyes and view life from a larger perspective? Or are you sucked into the chaos around you? In other words, are you able to stay the course in spite of what is occurring around you, or are you easily rocked by your circumstances?

Did you notice the answers I presented to my ten questions in Chapter Three: Questions Answered are grounded in the Bible? I meet more people who *don't* read or study their Bibles, than people who *do*—even among Christians. This concerns me greatly. For one, when tough times come there is no memory bank of verses that can be called to mind. Second, in order to sort out things that affect us and others, we have a propensity to use the grid with which we are accustomed. In short, we interpret and process our experiences through knowledge we have already accumulated. Without knowledge of the Bible, we are unable to process our circumstances through its contents. We are left with our own understandings of concepts such as "holy," "loving," and "God."

What has formed the grid through which you currently view the world? Has formulation of that grid been left to happenstance? Has your grid developed as a result of life experiences over which you have had little control? I don't know about you, but I want to be the one who selects the lens through which I view the world, and I am keenly interested in making sure I interpret events with as little error as possible. This interest leaves me aching to know the Bible so I can see things clearly.

Sadly, I am learning that many people don't strive to know the Bible because they believe it is one of many books they can consult for spiritual guidance. I contend that the Bible is set apart from all other books that speak of spiritual matters. According to 2 Timothy 3:16, "All Scripture is God-breathed and is useful for teaching, rebuking, correcting and training in righteousness, so that the man of God may be thoroughly equipped for every good work." The Bible is no ordinary book. Once it is read, once it is ingested, God uses it to change us. Notice the link in 2 Timothy 3:16 between knowing the Bible and being *thoroughly* equipped for *every* good work. We cannot live a life that displays God's strength and beauty without turning the pages of our Bible on a regular basis, paying close attention to what we read, and then living what it says.

You don't believe the Bible? I know there are many people who don't. I was greatly influenced by a man named Josh McDowell who set out to disprove Christianity and found he couldn't. His book, *Evidence that Demands a Verdict*, contains so much research material it has earned a spot on my shelf for decades as a regularly consulted reference book.[1] Some of McDowell's facts about the continuity of the Bible are so amazing that just having them on my bookshelf was unacceptable; so, I printed them out and taped the facts inside the cover of my Bible!

The facts about continuity between the sixty-six books of the Bible are as follows:

1. Written over a 1,500-year span.
2. Written over forty generations.
3. Written by over forty authors belonging to the most diverse walks of life.
4. Written in different places—various lands from west to east.
5. Written at different times—war and peace.
6. Written during different moods—some from heights of joy and others from the depth of sorrow and despair.
7. Written on three continents—Asia, Africa, and Europe.
8. Written in three languages—Hebrew, Aramaic, and Greek.
9. Its subject matter includes hundreds of controversial subjects.[2]

After outlining the above points in his book, Josh tells about a man who came to his house to recruit salesmen for the *Great Books of the Western World* series. In order to get the visitor to consider the Bible as a "Great Book," Josh posed the following challenge to the man. Imagine selecting just ten of the forty authors of the Bible, all from *one* walk of life, *one* generation, *one* place, *one* time, who are experiencing the same *one* mood, who all live on *one* continent, and are asked to write about *one* controversial subject. Would those authors agree even on *one* shared topic?[3] The answer is, "Of course not!" The books would be as varied in approach and thought as the authors themselves.

Yet look at the Bible. First written amidst diverse time periods, by diverse authors, in diverse locations and languages, the Bible's continuity is so astounding, it can be considered miraculous. So much so, that the visitor Josh challenged with this line of questioning committed his life to Christ two days later. As Josh writes, "Any person sincerely seeking truth would at least consider a book with the above qualifications."[4]

Within the theme of God's larger, unfolding story, we can identify various threads that begin in the book of Genesis and continue throughout the Bible and into the book of Revelation. Imagine the threads as part of a beautiful tapestry overhead that spans the ages. One thread is God's pursuit of people. Remember God pursuing Adam and Eve? In addition, we have seen hints of a dot-and-string thread showing us that life is short and eternity is long. We have also begun to uncover a "restored earth" thread. We see this in the fact that the garden of Genesis foreshadows the restored earth in Revelation. There we will enjoy God forever in an Eden-like environment. An additional thread is that Satan's activities have remained securely contained in a dot—even to the very day you read this page. They will remain in that dot until this age ends and Satan is thrown into hell forever. Once we develop eyes for spotting threads, we will never cease to discover them.

The number of threads that connect the Bible from beginning to end are too numerous to count. In fact, they qualify the Bible as a never-ending source of refreshment, understanding, and knowledge. In 1 Peter 1:24–25, we read, "All men are like grass, and all their glory is like the flowers of the field; the grass withers and the flowers fall, but the word of the Lord stands forever." If we continue to open the pages of God's Word and read with care, we will *never* stop experiencing its blessings, and we'll discover more about the cohesive tapestry called *God's Story.*

Though our lives are like grass compared to eternity, we can live them with strength and beauty. To prove my point, I would like to take a look at Psalm 1:1–3, beginning with verse three: "He is like a tree planted by streams of water, which yields its fruit in season and whose leaf does not wither. Whatever he does prospers." I want to look like that! No matter what my circumstances, I want to remain so connected to God that I never wither. I want to display the character of Christ every minute. I want to yield the fruit of the Spirit—love, joy, peace, patience, kindness, goodness, faithfulness, gentleness, and self-control (Galatians 5:22–23).

The secret for living a fruitful life as discussed in Psalm 1:3 is found in Psalm 1:2: "But his delight is in the law of the Lord, and on his law he meditates day and night." Ah, knowing God's word is key to living a fruitful life. Not a cursory short reading of verses here and there, but delighting in the Bible and pondering what it says. I mean cherishing, thinking, studying, memorizing, and praying that our lives line up with Psalm 1:3 and God's Word in general. Then our lives will reflect Him.

In addition to meditating on God's Word, the second key to a life of strength and beauty is to obey His Word. Psalm 1:1 says, "Blessed is the man who does not walk in the counsel of the wicked or stand in the way of sinners or sit in the seat of mockers. But his delight is in the law of the Lord . . ." A person who is *delighting* in the Bible (not just reading it) longs to live a life of purity and does not walk with the wicked. David says, "I have kept my feet from every evil path so that I might obey your word" (Psalm 119:101). The two go hand in hand. Knowing the Bible inspires new attitudes and behaviors. We change.

The Bible allows our eyes to rise up and see things from God's vantage point—from up above looking down, rather than from down here looking up. In its pages, we learn how we can join His story by living for things that last for eternity instead of living for purposes in the dot. From cover to cover, we learn that God is pursuing all of us because He wants us to know Him as well as He knows us. He also wants to shine through us to the world; therefore, He has given us a book so we can be "thoroughly equipped for every good work" (2 Timothy 3:16). The Bible offers wisdom for making decisions, inspiration for living well, promises to trust, warnings to protect us, and truth that enables us to discern lies. In the pages of our Bible, we learn that our eternal relationship with God isn't something that happens later; it has already begun.

In Chapter Three: Questions Answered, I scratched the surface in answering ten important questions regarding the chaos we experience in life. By digging deeper into the Bible, not only do we learn about God's story, we receive deeper insights and answers to questions such as I have discussed above. As we read and study the Bible, God mightily uses it to build a "grid" through which we can view life in new and clearer ways. This grid will help to keep chaos in its place.

To learn to live ABOVE the chaos, the order in which we consider information is as important as the information itself. When our eyes look up to see the perfect, powerful, eternal, and historical story unfurling above our heads, we gain *perspective.* That perspective—seeing the world from above—fuels the desire to enter the *process* that enables our hearts to become clean and pure so we look more like Christ. It is only when our hearts are clean and pure that we are able to love *people* with God's brand of love. Let's journey together to explore the perspective process, and people categories. Let's rise above the chaos that surrounds us by aligning our lives with the eternal purposes God is showing through "His Story."

Part Three

Perspective: How Should We View Our Lives?

Chapter Five

As a Firework

> You are the light of the world. A city on a hill cannot be hidden.
>
> —Matthew 5:14

Those of us with less than 20/20 vision need assistance to see clearly, whether it is in the form of eyeglasses, contacts, Lasik surgery, or "readers" purchased at the local drugstore. It's the same with perspective. Sometimes the way we view and process the world is warped because we are missing information or are using an inaccurate lens through which to view our lives. I hope you turned the last page because you have found some answers to common questions and that those answers have started to change the way you view the world. They certainly changed mine.

My eyes now see:

- God's relentless pursuit of all mankind from the moment He asked, "Where are you?" in the garden of Eden.

- God has been telling a larger, unstoppable story through history. I can choose whether or not to join in His story, but the story will continue regardless of what I decide.
- God loves me. He settled that matter 2,000 years ago when He died on the cross for me and then rose from the dead. This resounding victory was for us all. Jesus should receive our trust as the only way to eternal life.
- God's safety. His relentless, protective, pursuing love is keeping *history* safe, and it is keeping *me* safe since I placed my faith in Christ alone for my salvation.

Now, in Part Three – Perspective: How Should We View Our Lives?, we will explore ways in which God views each of us as we strive to be bright lights in a dark world. Some of the lenses I present in this part will resonate with you more than others, but all of them apply to each of us. The first lens is that of a firework.

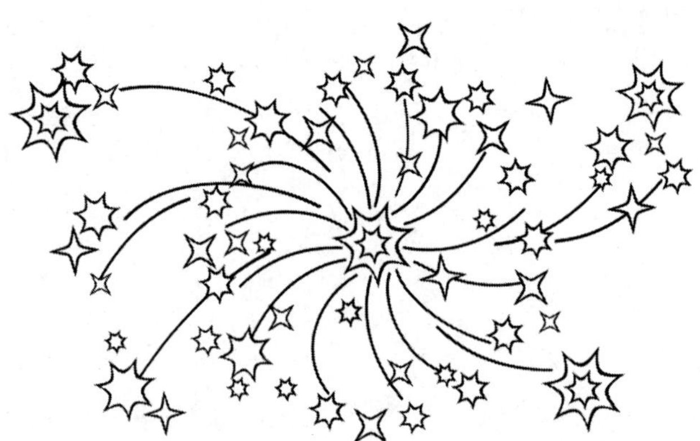

When my children were little, they asked when their birthday was. Though I could tell them the date, they had no idea what that meant in terms of how much time had to pass before their special day. To solve that problem, I taught them that when pumpkin stands begin to appear along roadsides, they would know their autumn birthday was very close. I looked forward to the squeals of delight that filled the car at the first pumpkin stand sighting each year.

What pumpkins were to my little girls, the Fourth of July has always been to me, because my birthday is celebrated a few days later. In the year 2000, God used a fireworks display to change my heart forever.

A friend invited a group of us to view fireworks at a private club. We loaded up towels and refreshments and made ourselves comfortable in a pristine golf course setting. Darkness fell upon the summer scene, and the fireworks display began. Because of the small crowd and safe environment for my children, I relaxed and enjoyed the beauty of the night sky more than I had in over a decade. The combination of arrangement, color, and types of fireworks was stunningly beautiful against the pitch-black canopy above.

My heart began to physically ache with longing as I watched the splendor exploding above my head. I found myself praying, actually begging for God to use me as a light for Him once again. An understanding exploded within my own heart that remains with me to this day. The parallel is obvious, I know, but it wasn't until that Fourth of July that my heart grabbed this truth and held on: *God is using Christians to make a light show that displays His splendor against the backdrop of a dark world.*

Each firework that evening had a different personality. I remember some that gently exploded high in the sky into giant powder puff shapes, but then quietly produced another layer of smaller puffs that cascaded softly from the first ones. At one point, I distinctly remember the outline of a blue star in the lower left-hand corner of the sky. It was soundless, short and sweet, but I remember it. Whoever designed that show had considered the individual characteristics of each firework, and launched each one at *just the right time* and in *just the right place* for the optimum beauty of the show as a whole.

There are currently 196 countries in the world, and the earth's population today is over seven billion people. Christians around the globe are firing off their individual lights for Christ as I write these words, and I have no way of knowing what it looks like to God as He looks down from a heavenly vantage point. I can only trust my holy and loving God, the firework arranger, to create a show that in its entirety is perfect and magnificent.

For the first time in my life that night, I didn't want to be anyone else in the universe. I suddenly understood that God had launched me into history at just the right time (my birthday) and in just the right place (my address) as part of His exquisite "light show." For the first time, I didn't want to trade places with people I admire—my personal heroes of faith. Though their "lights" are magnificent, I comprehended that God's light show would be changed without my light placed in the dark sky. Since God's firework plans are both perfect and perfectly executed, any changes interfering with God's design would make history less perfect, less brilliant.

Mother Teresa had a similar view about her role in history; she saw herself as part of the whole. She frequently spoke of her work as "just a drop in the ocean." About which she explained, "But if that drop was not in the ocean, I think the ocean would be less."[1] That night, under the stars, I got it. If I tried to emulate anyone else's light or path, there would be a hole where I was supposed to have fired in history. Also, if I am cranky about the role selected for me, I am like the kind of firework that makes its way up high in the sky, distracting us with its loud sputtering, but then disappointing us with its fizzle.

You can trust God too. Whether you relate most to a firework, a drop of water in an ocean, or perhaps a musical note in a symphony, know this: *you play a part in a beautiful display of God's splendor worldwide.* To fight that role, to quit and decide not to show up, dims the beauty of the overall show.

God picked your address and birthday.

> From one man he made every nation of men that they should inhabit the whole earth; and *he determined the times set for them and the exact places where they should live.* God did this so that men would seek him and perhaps reach out for him and find him though he is not far from each of us.
>
> —Acts 17:26, emphasis added

God is the only One who knows when, where, and how each firework of a Christian is to be shot into the sky for the show to reach its maximum beauty. Therefore, we can trust Him with our birth dates and addresses. As for me, I was born on July 7, 1961. I was launched into God's firework display when I became a Christian in the fall of 1973. The type of light I am (His character cast through my personality, strengths, weaknesses, and body frame) is perfect for the overall beauty of the show as well. I can trust God (the firework arranger) with that fact.

"However, as it is written: 'No eye has seen, no ear has heard, no mind has conceived what God has prepared for those who love him'—but God has revealed it to us by His Spirit" (1 Corinthians 2:9–10).

When we Christians decide to put our lights on stands as Christ followers, instead of hiding them under bowls, God does with our lives what we can never imagine in our wildest dreams. Simply put, God will write a more brilliant story with our lives—and our eternity—than we can ever write for ourselves.

I have received a large amount of biblical instruction from Christian women by way of DVDs, books, Bible studies, and the Internet. It amazes me how much I feel I know some of these individuals even though I have never met them! I used to think the best lights were the famous ones like Billy Graham, Ann Graham Lotz, Beth Moore, Corrie ten Boom, Deitrich Bonhoeffer, Joni Eareckson Tada . . . The list goes on. Since I have completed so many Bible studies by Beth Moore, let's pick her as an example of someone well-known, who is a light in this world for Jesus Christ. Do I want to grow up and be like her? Prior to my fireworks night, the honest answer was "yes." I wanted to grow up and be just like her, and all the other "famed lights" I just mentioned. But now I think differently. I know now that each light for Christ is *equal* in beauty.

Light #1: Beth Moore

Beth founded *Living Proof Ministries* in 1994, and has written numerous books and Bible studies that have benefited women of all ages, races, and denominations. She travels regularly to speak at conferences attended by thousands of people. When an expanded audience made possible by technology is counted, it becomes impossible to calculate the number of people to whom she has spoken. In the past, when I looked at Beth, whom I consider to be a brilliant light for Christ, I wondered: *How can I, Laurie O'Connor, compete with that?*

Let's now look at Beth's background through God's eyes. Here's what Beth has told about herself at various speaking engagements. She came from a rough background that left her with little trust in anything or anyone. In childhood, she was fearful of nearly everything, and exhibited destructive behaviors as she grappled with the stresses she faced.

Beth is where she is today because she chose to trust her heavenly Father, and took steps of faith that terrified her. Step-by-step, she made room for God to write a stunning story for Himself if He wanted to, and of course, He always wants to! Consider how God felt when she was making all those private steps prior to her fame, when no one else was looking but Him. I know what He was doing. With every one of Beth's steps, God smiled, God cheered, and God rushed in to fill the space she made for Him to show His glory.

Light #2: Cheryl Burton

Years ago, my friends Ray and Sue partnered with Dan and Cheryl to provide disaster relief in Granada through the Billy Graham Association. Cheryl was in her sixth year of battling cancer. She received a chemo treatment just before she left on the trip. Ray has a leg afflicted with polio.

The night they left, I lay my head on my pillow even as these four individuals—one with cancer, one with polio, and all of them retired—were flying to Grenada somewhere in the sky. I thought: *There's no more beautiful sight in the world right now than those four people, and the world doesn't even know about them!* I think I experienced God's heart. Each of those individuals had a reason to stay home, but they chose instead to slip anonymously through the night sky on a mission. I think God was beside Himself with glee as those four made room for Him to write a stunning story if He wanted to, and of course, He always wants to! They were bright lights in His show that night. God smiled, God cheered, and God rushed in to fill the space they made for Him to show His glory.

Cheryl went to see Jesus face-to-face at 1:00 p.m. on April 23, 2008. Her daughter wrote in an e-mail announcement, "Heaven became sweeter today." I have no doubt that is true.

Light #3: Me

Nobody knows me. I am a mom of two girls in college while their little brother, who is still in elementary school, wonders why the house is now so quiet. I have four stepchildren and two step-grandbabies. I am not famous. I am not serving the Lord in any ministry you would hear about. I am an instructor at a junior college, not a famous university. I am a mom doing the mundane. For years, I have worked on a book not certain it would ever go to print. In spite of that, I typed because I believed God wanted me to share what He taught me, and I knew I was making room for Him to do something for Himself if He wanted to.

I believe He smiled as I wrote. I believe He cheered. You are reading this today because He rushed in to fill the spaces these pages made for Him to show His glory.

Have you noticed the common thread running between these completely different lights? Each made *conscious decisions* to give God room to work. Each put her light on a stand in order to do something God-sized—something for His sake only and in His strength alone.

> Neither do people light a lamp and put it under a bowl. Instead they put it on its stand, and it gives light to everyone in the house. In the same way, let your light shine before men, that they may see your good deeds and praise your Father in heaven.
>
> —Matthew 5:14–15

We should not compare the heart decisions that each of these people made to create room for God. And we cannot determine that one decision was more valuable than another. At their roots, the decisions were the same—abandoning a story they would have written for themselves in order to make room for God's more meaningful story. The decisions also required courage and risk-taking. For us, the decision to make space for God is equally hard. If we make the room, He will rush in and do something different through each of us, but the overall result will be His maximum glory. Such decisions require courageous trust. We will be risking something bigger than ourselves so God can use us if He wants to, and of course, He always wants to!

I want to point out that it is possible for people with impure hearts to decide to do a great act for God, and to ask Him to bless it. This is not what I am alluding to. I am talking about people with clean, pure, and changed hearts that make room for God to use them. God-led hearts produce God-guided actions so in the end, God gets credit for all of it.

With this distinction in mind, let us understand that to be a light means to provide room for God to operate, and to risk opening up space in your relationships for Him to do something with them if He wishes. If I don't mention Jesus in my relationships with people, I am not giving Him space to operate in those relationships.

Paul wrote most of the New Testament in the form of letters to churches. While in prison for his faith, Paul ended a letter with the following plea.

> Pray also for me, that whenever I open my mouth, words may be given me so that I will fearlessly make known the mystery of the gospel,

> for which I am an ambassador in chains. Pray that I may declare it fearlessly, as I should.
>
> —Ephesians 6:19–20

There is a strong indication in these verses that Paul was fearful or, at the very least, tempted to hide his light for Christ under a bowl. This is a decision every Christ-follower must make as discussed in Chapter Three—"Why are we here?"—yet, look at what God did with the room this man gave Him. God smiled. God cheered. God rushed in to fill the space Paul made for Him to show His glory. Paul most likely had no idea his letters would become part of the Bible. But his courageous decisions resulted in a life story he could have never envisioned, verbalized, or planned. He was a light that fired and glorified God.

Lights are firing around the world, and they are *all* beautiful, *all* spectacular, and *all* meaningful. None is more valuable than the other, because at the root, each Christian makes the same heart decision to create room for God, and to put His light on a stand for people to see. Just like I have no idea what He is ultimately doing with my life, I have no idea what He is ultimately doing with anyone else's. My children, friends, and husband each have a different role to play in God's story. They are their own lights for Christ and are led to different places in the dark sky than where I am headed. I must let them be the expressions of Christ He has made them to be.

How have these understandings changed me as a mom? When John and I married, we created a blended family. He already had four beautiful children, and I was pregnant with two more. Eventually our third child arrived. As a result, all of our children have dealt with the hellos and good-byes inherent in having half-brothers and sisters and half-nieces and nephews. During extended visits, the kids get reacquainted only to say good-bye again. Sometimes a sibling lives with us for a season. We reconfigure bedrooms, accommodate another person into our routine, and then, the sibling leaves again—another good-bye.

I can fret and worry over the constant and extreme changes in relationships that our children experience. Or I can trust God with the light He wants them to ultimately be in this dark world. In the future, I can picture them able to "roll with the punches," accommodate change, welcome guests, and handle roommates with style and grace. Their whole lives have been a training ground for such things. It's not a training ground I am creating in an effort for them to turn out a certain way; it's something God is up to. God intervenes with circumstances that come from His hand either because He arranges them or allows them.[2] He is in the process of including my children in His story at the exact places and times their individual capacities can shine best for His maximum glory. I can only embrace their journeys as I am simultaneously walking through mine.

How has this understanding of God's fireworks display changed me as a wife? Like me, my husband is a light for Christ and invited to participate in God's story. When he makes room for God too, his light is glorious. My husband's heart drives him to deliver Easter baskets to police officers, firefighters, and the elderly. He delivers dinners and grocery money to the needy and sick. And because of my husband, our family has done volunteer work at a home for abused children. Though I participate wholeheartedly with him in these endeavors, I can tell you not one of them would be happening if it weren't for him. I am not naturally driven to do this type of worthwhile work. But, if I made the mistake of interfering with his light for Christ by squelching his desires and ideas through things like complaining or discouraging words, the light show for God would be dimmed.

Unlike in the earlier days of our marriage, I now have little to say about John's life, and how I think it should look. I am learning that John has to answer to God for his life, and I answer to God for mine. My responsibility is to continue to know God better and to display Him more beautifully with each passing day of life (Isaiah 60:21), and *nothing* has to interfere with my ability to do so.

I used to believe that other people and circumstances could jeopardize my ability to live my best for God. Since I didn't feel in control of my own destiny, I was threatened by all that went on around me, which meant I felt vulnerable and unsafe. As a result, I was overly concerned with how others lived their lives, and found myself inappropriately trying to control circumstances.

Over time, my sense of safety has shifted to the overarching story God is telling. He is in charge of my destiny. God has me living *now*, not 100 years ago. He has me living in *Georgia*, not Texas. He gave me *these* children, not anyone else's. I am married to *this* husband, not someone else's. The same God Who is relentlessly protecting history's story is also protecting *mine.* Nothing will stop that story from happening. We just need to relax and let Him tell it through us.

God used the fireworks display over a country club lawn in Georgia to explode within me realizations about my unique role in "His Story" and the meticulous timing and placement of my life on the globe. I hope the fireworks display visual has gotten you thinking about your significant light in history and about how beautiful you are as a firework in God's light show. I hope you are inspired to participate in a way that will maximize the show's beauty.

If you are not yet a Christian, please do not be tempted to think you can adopt this firework perspective and somehow make it work for you. Being part of this story is a blessing Christians receive through a personal relationship with Jesus Christ. Our light comes from the Holy Spirit living inside of us. As our lives transform from within, the Spirit works through us to change the world around us. The results are ultimately so dramatic and beautiful that no human being can take the credit for them. What happens is clearly God's handiwork.

Tonight, as I review these words, I remember my son's life verse. "For we have this treasure in jars of clay to show that this all surpassing power is from God, not men" (2 Corinthians 4:7). May it be that not only my son, but every Christian, lives a life so grand that the only thing people can say is, "That person's life cannot be attributed to human effort; it can only be credited to God."

Chapter Six

As a Picture Frame

> For you created my inmost being; you knit me together in my mother's womb. I praise you because I am fearfully and wonderfully made; your works are wonderful, I know that full well. My *frame was not hidden* from you when I was made in the secret place. When I was woven together in the depths of the earth, your eyes saw my unformed body. All the days ordained for me were written in your book before one of them came to be.
>
> —Psalm 139:13–16, emphasis mine

The Hebrew word *'ōṣem* is translated as "frame" in the NIV. A more expanded meaning of *'ōṣem* is "framework."[1] In the context of Psalm 139:15, the framework being referred to is that of the human skeleton. As varied as human bodies are, they are all held up, supported, and shaped by skeletal frames that define height, arm and leg length, and facial structure. Each person's frame has been handcrafted by God.

My love for photography includes an appreciation for framing because the frame showcases the picture. The wrong frame diminishes the beauty of the image. I know I have found the correct frame when the picture suddenly looks stunning.

I recall working on a scrapbook for my mom and dad for Christmas one year. We had taken my parents to Ireland that summer. The sole purpose of the trip was to take my dad to visit the town in which his great-grandfather had lived, as well as to see the church he had attended. When it came time to scrapbook a photo I had taken of the church, I looked for a paper color on which to mount it. I tried several different colors, but was not satisfied—until I tried kelly-green. Suddenly, the photo was no longer a snapshot. It was a postcard-perfect photo of the church, taken on a glorious, sun-kissed, never-ending, blue-skied day in Ireland. The transformation was all about the framing.

Let's now apply this principle of the importance of framing art to the Artist Himself and to the way the Artist views you. God made your frame, and since He is perfect, He gave you the perfect frame for your part in His story. You look great in His frame. In *His* frame for you, you are a postcard reflection of Him. To be in any other frame would make *His* story less beautiful.

I can dye my hair, straighten my hair, curl my hair, or cut my hair. I can gain or lose weight, pierce my ears, or wear new make-up, but I am still recognizable because of the things about me I can't change. The way God formed my mouth, larynx, and vocal cords creates a voice distinctly my own. My height, gait, the line of my shoulders, and the shape of my body are distinct enough that I can be recognized from afar.

God also gave each of us particular personalities, capabilities, dreams, passions, and interests. Some might refer to these as elements of the "soul." Here, I will refer to these inner qualities as the "person." The "person," like the frame, can experience only limited change. As for myself, I love to learn, am analytical, have always been a morning person, and have an artistic side. I am not going to change those facets of myself. They are inherent, and they are showcased through my frame. There is no separating the "person" from the frame. We can trust that just like the snapshot I took in Ireland looked perfect in its frame, our individual frames combine with our individual persons to become postcard perfect reflections of Christ's character to the world around us.

American culture places much emphasis on the frame. I suspect people from every culture experience the pressure to value their frames more than intangible things such as their persons. We need to fight the urge to make the frame more important than the person. *Our frame has one purpose, and one purpose only—to be the showcase through which the world can see the person God has created us to be.*

One of our daughters was selected for homecoming court in her senior year. As my husband and I stood alongside her in the crisp fall air, I knew the only person qualified to judge who was believed to be the most beautiful *person* in the school was God Himself. I suspect some of the most beautiful people in the school were never even considered for a vote because "Man looks at the outward appearance. . ." (1 Samuel 16:7). We know from the remainder of the verse, however, that ". . . the Lord looks at the heart." We are not qualified to make determinations about that which only God can see—the person. Some students might have argued they cast their vote for the person, not the frame. Maybe so, but the vote was still cast based only on what was known. Everyone has a life hidden from public view, and only God can see what is done in secret (Matthew 6:4, 6, 18; Hebrews 4:12).

Even God acknowledges there are physically attractive people in the world. The Bible describes various men as notably good-looking. Joseph was "well built and handsome" (Genesis 39:6). David was "ruddy, with a fine appearance and handsome features" (1 Samuel 16:12). As far as women: the "Egyptians saw that (Sarai) was a beautiful woman" (Genesis 12:14); Rebekah "was very beautiful" (Genesis 24:16); and Rachel was "lovely in form and beautiful" (Genesis 29:17). Our eyes do indeed see levels of beauty. It's not our imagination. But the point of this section is *no matter what your level of beauty determined by society, you are encased in the perfect frame for the story God has for you.*

Did you know God didn't even pick a handsome frame for His Son, Jesus?

> He grew up before him like a tender shoot, and like a root out of dry ground. He had no beauty or majesty to attract us to him, nothing in his appearance that we should desire him.
>
> —Isaiah 53:2

Nothing about Jesus Christ's appearance would make us desire Him or be drawn to Him. Why would God put His precious Son in a frame that drew no attention whatsoever? Perhaps so that no one could ever say people followed Him because He was handsome. Whatever the reason, it is safe to assume that Christ's frame was selected based on what was best for God's story. In this case, God's best was that Jesus be in a body that gave us no reason to look at Him. Because of this prime example, we can know that attractiveness is not needed to live a revolutionary life. In fact, a "lack" of attractiveness in one person is as purposeful and handpicked a plan as attractiveness for another person.

After considering this matter heavily, I have concluded that I want my *person* to be in the frame God has selected for me—the frame that will most reflect His character to the world. If given the choice, I would look over all of the options and then look at God and say, "You pick." I see the reflection of what He picked in the mirror. The perfect frame to showcase God through me is five-foot-seven inches tall with brown hair, freckled skin, green eyes, and long arms.

No matter what my level of beauty according to society's standards, I choose to embrace my frame as personally knitted by God. Outward appearance never excuses us from living full-tilt in both character and purpose.

As we ponder the idea that our frames play a role in how God's character is reflected to the world, one may ask, "What about genetic 'glitches?'" Life under the curse includes disease, sickness, and death. And it's heartbreaking. There are no words to describe the pain that produces the heart-wrenching sobs, the deep dark holes of depression, or the self-protective numbing that can occur when the chaos of illness is incessant. Satan approached Eve in the garden of Eden as a predator whose intent was to "steal and kill and destroy" (John 10:10). But God pursued us immediately with: "Where are you?" As we reviewed in Chapter Three—"Why did Dan die early?"—the chaos—including that of illness and disability—is confined to a dot. God remains in control at all times. It's in dark times, when chaos is attempting to wrestle us to the ground, that we must fight to trust His story, both for history and for each individual. His story is always good and always reigns supreme. So if your frame has been changed by illness or injury, please know that God sees your pain. He wants to press in closer to you with assurance that your value in His story remains *exactly* the same as it was before your illness. If you or someone you love has been born with illness or disability, please be confident that God's story is not limited by genetics and that the frame is good for you, the afflicted, and for the story God is telling.

I know people whose frames have been changed by disease or illness, but they choose to let the person God made them shine through *no matter what.* In so doing, they remain effectual, productive, radiant people used for God's story on earth.

My friend, Linda Byrd, has already gone to be with the Lord. She started to have trouble with her legs in high school and was diagnosed with multiple sclerosis. The disease progressed to the point that she became bedridden.

Linda loved Jesus. Her eyes brightened when visitors entered the room. She would say, "I love you," even though it was difficult to form words. Christmas cards were sent and signed with her beautiful, wriggly "X." Joni Eareckson Tada has spent years examining the glory God receives when the disabled choose to love Jesus when their frames fail them. In her book, *A Quiet Place in a Crazy World*, Joni points out that when no one else is watching, angels are. What a show Linda was putting on for the angels in heaven! They must have been thinking that if God can inspire that kind of devotion, He must be awesome. The angels may have then turned to worship God for His greatness.[2]

During the last ten years of her life—between 1993 and 2003—Linda's light was firing into the sky. I am sorry you missed it. Jesus looked spectacular in her. God saw it, however, along with the angels in heaven and all who knew her. What the curse did to her genetics, God spun for His glory because His story reigns. Linda's dot is over, and she is alive and well for all of eternity.

Joni Eareckson Tada is another person who lives magnificently for God within her frame. She has had a huge impact on my life, but you probably know that due to the number of times she is cited in this book. A diving accident in 1967 left Joni, then seventeen, as a quadriplegic in a wheelchair. Today, Joni is an artist who paints with her mouth, is an author of many books, and is the founder of *Joni and Friends International Disability Center*. Her work as an international advocate for people with disabilities has taken her to forty-five countries. Today, she continues the life she has built alongside her husband, Ken Tada, since 1982.

But I don't want you to become distracted by the bio. I want you to see Joni's decision to never stop being the *person* God made her to be, no matter what happened to her *frame*. It is that *decision* that led to her bio. It is also that *decision* that has influenced my life through her writing. She *let* her frame determine that she would serve the worldwide community of the disabled.

Do my examples communicate that everyone is a more powerful light for God when his or her frame is disabled? Not at all. I share these two examples to push back against the tidal wave of what society wants us to believe: that a person's frame is extremely important; that some frames are better than others; that a person's frame determines value; and that a person's frame can limit how beautiful his or her life can become.

People like Linda and Joni take away the excuses of the majority of us with "normal" frames who think our light for Jesus is somehow hindered by a large nose or wide hips. We too can learn to make the same exact decision Linda and Joni made. *We can decide that our frames will not stop God's strong and beautiful story from being told with our lives.* Further, we can trust that our frames were handpicked by God as the perfect showcase for exhibiting the person God created us to be. When we get to heaven one day, we too will see that our frames in this dot of a life were an integral part of the glorious story God was penning all along.

Chapter Seven

As a Mathematician

The kingdom of heaven is like a mustard seed . . .

—Matthew 13:31

You might be thinking: *No, Laurie! I hate numbers, math, and calculations. I want to skip this!*

Please don't.

One of my daughters struggles with the idea that Christians are the lights of the world. When she looks around her twenty-something world, she sometimes sees people who *aren't* Christians living "brighter" lives than people who *are* Christians. "Mom," she says, "they are living a good life too!"

I think of people like Albert Einstein, Thomas Edison, Alexander Graham Bell, and the Wright Brothers who exercised their brilliant minds and ingenuity to provide the precursors of the comforts we enjoy today. I don't know what the spiritual condition of their hearts were, but I do know they changed the world beyond their lifetimes. For those who did not know Christ, however, the good produced by their lives is only going to last for a dot of time. Let me explain.

I first proposed that a single life span could be represented by a dot on a string. I later explained that all of Satan's activities are also contained in that same tiny dot (see "Why did Dan die early?" and "Who is Satan?"). Now adding further dimension to the dot-string concept, each contribution of the brilliant historic figures just named is a dot. In fact, the entire timespan of world history is a dot. Absolutely *everything* shrinks to nothingness compared to eternity—the never-ending, ever-widening, unfathomable span of forever.

> Lift up your eyes to the heavens, look at the earth beneath; the heavens will vanish like smoke, the earth will wear out like a garment, and its inhabitants die like flies. But my salvation will last forever, my righteousness will never fail.
>
> —Isaiah 51:6

The earth is going to wear out. Right now, there is a huge movement aimed at taking care of our earth. I am very concerned about taking care of our earth for future generations and using our resources carefully. I am still influenced by a summer I spent in the Philippines when I was nineteen. There I was introduced to a simpler lifestyle. I often stand in American department stores and grocery stores and beg God's forgiveness for the stockpiles of clothes and food items that will never be used. As concerned as I am, however, such efforts will only delay the inevitable. The earth is going to wear out, and God is going to make all things new again for those who have a relationship with Him.

> Behold, I will create new heavens and a new earth. The former things will not be remembered, nor will they come to mind . . . I will rejoice over

> Jerusalem and take delight in my people; the sound of weeping and of crying will be heard in it no more.
>
> —Isaiah 65:17, 19

Your life can connect to eternity if you want it to, or you can just spend it on stuff that lasts for a speck in time. The choice is yours. You tap into God's story the moment you establish a personal relationship with Jesus Christ. From then on, you participate in God's story by inviting Him to write His story through you if He wants to—and He always wants to.

Time is flying by. God is asking us to give Him a penny (our years). In return, He will give us a million dollars (eternity). He is asking us to give Him a pinpoint in time, and He'll give us forever. God is explosive in His returns. He compared the kingdom of heaven to a mustard seed. "Though it is the smallest of all seeds, when it grows, it is the largest of garden plants and becomes a tree, so that the birds of the air come and perch on its branches" (Matthew 13:32).

God is always doing what I now call "mustard seed math." Jesus fed thousands with a few fish and loaves . . . twice . . . with leftovers! (Matthew 14:13–21; Mark 6:31–44; Luke 9:10–17; John 6:5–15). Such results can only be attributed to the kingdom of heaven.

God asked Moses to stretch out his hand over the sea; then He drove the sea back with a strong east wind (Exodus 14:21). Moses stretched out his hand over the sea again, and at daybreak, the sea went back to its place (Exodus 14:27). God asked Joshua to organize a procession led by a trumpet-blowing marching band and commanded them to march around Jericho seven times. Immediately thereafter, God made the walls of Jericho come tumbling down (Joshua 6:1–21).

If God parted the Red Sea with one man's outstretched arm and crumbled city walls with an army's circular march and trumpet blowing, what will God do with the dollar bills you give to support a teenager's mission trip to Africa? What will God do with the time you spend with a neighbor over tea talking transparently about both your common day-to-day activities as well as your spiritual life? God clearly demonstrates in the Bible that whatever action He asks us to take for Him will *shrink* in comparison to what He then does with it for His name.

If we live in God's strength and for His purposes, instead of our own, God will do things with our lives that cannot be explained by human calculations. Watch someone trusting God with the addition of a family member, or parents trusting God with a child's illness, or a woman trusting God with marital heartbreak, or a father trusting God with unemployment, and you will see something beyond the mathematical predictions of this world. When this happens, you know you are watching something from heaven, and that it is not those who are struggling who should be praised, but the God who sustains them.

God's math is the only math I like. It's the best deal in town. I honestly have no clue why anyone would turn Him down. He first makes a way for us to be rescued from eternal darkness, and then He gives us the chance to include our dot in a calculation that never fails to produce remarkable results.

I have spoken about our oldest daughter, Elizabeth, who moved in with us because she was struggling to work and go to school on her own. We carried on with our normal lives while Elizabeth finished college nearby and worked full-time at a restaurant. But with an eye toward eternity, one day I took her to lunch for an hour and brought up the topic of Jesus. I explained how she could know Him personally, drawing diagrams on a napkin. Then later there was an opportunity to send her on a college retreat, which we did.

At that retreat, she prayed to receive Jesus Christ as her personal Savior with a man named Louie Giglio.

Today, Elizabeth is married to a Christian man and raising her children in a home where God is talked about as a matter of course and the Bible is taught regularly. How much did I invest in Elizabeth's life? I prayed for her regularly over the years, offered her our home to continue college more comfortably, managed some of her medical and dental care, took her for lunch at a Mexican restaurant, and spent some money to send her on a retreat. What did God do with those meager, doable, simple offerings of my life? Amazing things. Absolutely amazing mustard-seed-math results occurred from our efforts to help Elizabeth grasp matters of eternity. We could have chosen to focus on keeping her comfortable and happy for this dot of time, but because she came to know Jesus, she lives transparently as a Christian in her home, at her job, in her neighborhood, and with the women in her church. Some of what she does now will literally last forever.

How does the dot perspective change the way I live? Since life is short, I must decide how to spend it. Do you want to invest your dot in things that last for only an earthly lifetime? I don't. Houses, couches, landscaping, jobs, schooling . . . They all serve a purpose, but they cease to exist when I do (or sooner). I want to invest in a life that counts for God. How about you? Everyone who trusts in Jesus becomes part of God's calculator. As we let Him press the buttons, the results will be remarkable.

> Now to him who is able to do immeasurably more than all we ask or imagine, according to his power that is at work within us, to him be glory in the church and in Christ Jesus throughout all generations, for ever and ever! Amen.
>
> —Ephesians 3:20–21

Chapter Eight

As a Soldier

> Endure hardship with us like a good soldier of Christ Jesus. No one serving as a soldier gets involved in civilian affairs—he wants to please his commanding officer.
>
> —2 Timothy 2:3–4

Looking back, I believe I fell apart after Dan's death for two main reasons. First, I did not understand the spiritual battle taking place around me, and second, I did not know how to fight it. In my early years with Christ, I did not know the material about Satan presented in Chapter Three—"Who is Satan?" and "Why is Satan permitted to operate today?"

It took years for me to learn:

- about the revolt that had occurred in the heavens,
- how limited and temporary Satan's power is in light of eternity,

- that God's eternal story is being protected and kept safe,
- and that the history of the world and Satan's reign is as brief as the next blink of my eye.

As important as these understandings are, the most important piece I missed was that Satan's most common strategy is to *toss us lies at opportune times.* It never occurred to me when I was "logically" determining that God didn't love me because he "killed" my brother, that those thoughts were flaming arrows from Satan, who was actively trying to hinder me, distract me, and ruin me, so I would not be a light in God's story. Because I didn't know about this spiritual battle, I couldn't recognize the devil's work or stand against his attacks. In short, I did not see myself as a soldier.

Remember in the garden of Eden how Satan picked the most *crafty* animal of all *wild* animals through which to deceive Adam and Eve? Didn't it feel like there was an expert marksman who was taking well-planned, well-strategized, and well-aimed shots at the couple? We have learned the serpent was and is Satan.

The Bible tells us how to live victoriously in spite of this insidious enemy. We are to be on guard (1 Peter 5:8) and resist the devil (James 4:7). In addition, we are to put on our *spiritual* armor because the battle we wage is *spiritual.* Take a look, and if you can, stand as you read this next passage of Scripture:

> Finally, be strong in the Lord and in his mighty power. Put on the full armor of God so that you can take your *stand* against the *devil's schemes.* For our struggle is not against flesh and blood, but against the rulers, against the authorities, against

> the powers of this dark world and *against the spiritual forces of evil* in the heavenly realms. Therefore, put on the full armor of God, so that when the day of evil comes, you may be able to *stand* your ground, and after you have done everything, to *stand. Stand* firm then, with the belt of truth buckled around your waist, with the breastplate of righteousness in place, and with your feet fitted with the readiness that comes from the gospel of peace. *In addition to all this, take up the shield of faith, with which you can extinguish all the flaming arrows of the evil one.* Take the helmet of salvation and the sword of the Spirit, which is the word of God, and pray in the Spirit on all occasions with all kinds of prayers and requests. With this in mind, be alert and always keep on praying for all the saints.
>
> —Ephesians 6:10–18, emphasis mine

I can understand God telling us to put on armor, but I wonder why He doesn't tell us to go out and ferociously wage battle. Instead, God asks us to stand. That doesn't seem very soldier-like. It's so . . . doable. We are to stand in truth and choose by faith to reject the flaming-arrow lies when they come our way.

I mentioned in Chapter Three—"Who is Satan?"—that the devil is spending his dot of time feverishly trying to thwart the kingdom of God in two ways. First, he does everything in his power to stop people from coming to know Jesus in the first place. Second, once a person becomes a Christian, Satan fights to keep him or her ineffective for God's purposes.

I believe I recently watched a young man in my life take a series of "hits" meant to keep him from hearing about Jesus in the first place. The young man had a sudden interest in developing his relationship with God and was excitedly expressing that interest to family and friends. *Within one week*, he missed a phone message inviting him to a church activity; he attended a party in town and met a woman who had *no* spiritual interests; and he was suddenly scheduled to work at his job on Sundays for the *very first time* since being hired. The brief flame of spiritual interest was gone in just a few days. It's as if someone came along and snatched away the interest. I believe that may be exactly what happened. Jesus warns: "When anyone hears the message about the kingdom and does not understand it, the evil one comes and snatches away what was sown in his heart" (Matthew 13:18–19).

It will always be a struggle to introduce people to the lifesaving message of Jesus, but never blame the people for the difficulties. Our struggles are never with people. Rather, our struggles are "against the spiritual forces of evil in the heavenly realms" (Ephesians 6:12). Keep fighting, because Satan loses the "salvation battle" frequently.

For example, Satan lost his battle with me when I became a Christian at twelve years old. I was "rescued from the dominion of darkness and brought into the kingdom of the Son he loves, in whom I have redemption, the forgiveness of sins" (Colossians 1:13–14). But once Satan lost the battle of keeping me from becoming a Christian (which meant he couldn't rob me of a perfect eternity any longer), he instead began to strategize about how to render me useless as a light for Jesus Christ with my dot of time. If you are a Christian, the same is true for you.

In her book, *Captivating*, Stasi Eldredge describes what Satan is up to with his brief amount of time.

> Satan and the fallen angels, now demons, have been cast down, but they are not chained. Not yet.

> Now, "Your enemy the devil prowls around like a roaring lion looking for someone to devour" (1 Peter 5:8). And he does devour. He assaults and maims and steals and kills and destroys wherever he can, and the brunt of his malice falls on God's image bearers. On you and me.[1]

In addition to the struggle we experience every day because of the curse that blankets every human being, Satan is taking well-aimed shots at anyone showing spiritual interest or living purposefully for God's kingdom. He aims lies at our most vulnerable systems of thinking and launches them on our most exhausted days. It is no accident that Satan tempted Jesus at the *end* of his forty-day fast in the wilderness (Matthew 4:3–11). Satan seeks opportunity then goes for the jugular with specific lies (Luke 22:3–4, 6).

Hindsight being what it is, I now see that a series of events leading up to Dan's death gave opportunity for Satan to take a well-aimed strike at my desperate need to feel loved by God and people. Because I had never learned about spiritual battles, I didn't have all of my spiritual armor on and could not withstand the assault.

Opportunity begins: A boyfriend breaks up with me

Just before Dan's death, I was in full-time Christian work on a college campus when I suffered a huge blow to my heart. The love of my life broke up with me. We had dated my junior and senior year of college, but he met someone else and fell in love with her. My heart shattered into a million pieces at the news. *Devastation* is the only descriptive word that applies unless there's such a thing as super-charged, extra traumatic devastation! Deep down, the undergirding of my heart became splintered by this event. The relationship had been completely honorable, so why didn't God let it work out? I started to wonder if God really loved me.

More opportunity: I was sent to counseling

I attended a mandatory counseling evaluation as part of my job on the same college campus, and was told I needed counseling. The counselor had tears in his eyes as he told me I had no idea what it meant to be loved. I had no idea what he meant by that, but trusted his insight. I was transferred to a college campus located near a reputable counselor with whom I met twice a week.

More opportunity: Exhaustion sets in

Several months later, after moving to a new campus, I was driving to a speaking engagement when I turned the car around and drove to my campus director's home instead. I literally curled up on his living room floor in the fetal position and sobbed my eyes out, telling him I never wanted to present another talk or lead another Bible study again. Yes, I had become so exhausted from trying so hard to please God with an *exceptional* life that I *quit* full-time Christian work soon after that night. In hindsight, I believe I grew weary of striving so hard for a God I wasn't certain loved me anymore. The splintering in my heart was worsening.

More opportunity: Dan and I get close

By some miracle, I got accepted into a master's degree program in Communication. During that time, Dan and I started getting very close. You already know he was taking a year off from college and living in New Jersey. I called him every Saturday at 1:30 p.m., and we talked for at least an hour. I loved Dan so much

I said a crazy sentence one day. I was talking to a friend about how much I loved my brother, and I said, "I could handle anything except my brother, Dan, dying." Nuts, I know. I couldn't have handled the death of my parents or younger brother either, but in that moment of realizing my love for my brother, I said those words.

More opportunity: Dan dies

Two weeks after saying that ridiculous sentence, Dan had his accident—right when I was feeling unloved, inadequate, and exhausted. On top of it all, I had been closer to my brother than ever before.

Returning to school after Dan's funeral, I was nothing more than pain with arms and legs. I was so weak a feather could have knocked me over, making me a prime target for continued confused thinking.

More opportunity: The ex-boyfriend enters again

Six months passed by, I was still reeling in pain when two things happened *within days of each other* that intensified the battle. First, I received a note from the college boyfriend who had shattered my heart, informing me that he was getting married the following month. *During the same week*, a friend at the university I was attending started expressing interest in me. I enjoyed this man's company, but we did not share spiritual interests.

I am not saying Satan was behind the succession of events—the raw pain of Dan's death, the handwritten reminder of past heartache, and the promise of a new relationship. However, I believe he saw my frailty and launched some carefully aimed lies in my direction to see if I would exchange them for the truth. Please remember, once Satan loses us to the kingdom of God, he then tries to render us useless for God's purposes. I believe Satan saw an opportunity to diminish my chances of ever being an effective light for Jesus Christ. He took two well-aimed shots at my greatest vulnerabilities in quick succession.

Flaming arrow #1: "God does not love you, Laurie."

Flaming arrow #2: "The Christian life is too hard, so quit."

I swallowed both false statements—hook, line, and sinker—and married that university friend after just *one date*, which allowed me to get to the marriage altar before my college boyfriend made it to his. Yes, you read that right. I purposed to get married before my ex-boyfriend did, and yes, my thinking was that contorted. People can be "baited" and their lives diverted when lies are received during vulnerable times.

The devil took well-aimed shots at a young, tired, insecure, naïve woman who was ill-equipped to see the battle raging around her. Her faith had splintered from a break-up that caused her to doubt God loved her. Following that, her faith grew tired of serving a God she doubted loved her. Then the final blow—her brother died. In her frail mind, that was three strikes for God. She foolishly excused herself from His ballgame.

I need to explain also that at this point in my life I had one close Christian friend but was not in community with any other Christians. I had no natural Christian support in my university relationships, and I did not invest the necessary energy to find Christian support in a local church or elsewhere. No soldier enters war alone. Soldiers engage in battle alongside comrades. I did not understand I needed the encouragement of a Christian community in order to stand firm (Hebrews 10:25). This lack of community further weakened my ability to battle well even as my thinking continued to spiral downward.

Thankfully, none of us has to become trained assassins or black belts in order to keep ourselves safe from such spiritual attacks. What wins the battle over the long haul is the *combination* of having a close relationship with God, the support of Christ-centered friendships, and choosing to believe the truth over the lies. We just need to stand in truth.

"Submit yourselves, then, to God. Resist the devil, and he will flee from you" (James 4:7). We resist the devil by never giving up on living in right relationship with God. We resist by fighting the "good fight" (2 Timothy 4:7). We fight to teach our children to trust God's plan even when we don't know His plan for them yet. We fight to maintain healthy relationships. We fight to give God time when the world demands we stay busy. We fight to stay connected to God when we feel He doesn't hear us. We fight to live by God's standards when the world is begging us to give in and give up. We fight to be a light in a world that rejects God. We fight to make decisions in light of the "string" when the world is screaming for us to live for the "dot."

If we have the mindset of a soldier, we can recognize the lies and combat them with the truth about God's story. We can keep our eyes fixed on our Commander-in-Chief, and not get swept up in civilian duties that take us out of the battleground. This helps us to live ABOVE the chaos.

Chapter Nine

As a Space Maker

> Your kingdom come, your will be done on earth as it is in heaven.
>
> —Matthew 6:10

Absolutely nothing stops God's grander story taking place overhead. We saw in the first half of this book that heaven will eventually take over and fill the earth again (Ephesians 1:9–10). We don't have to wait until the end of the story to get a taste of the kingdom of heaven, however. We can invite God's story to come down and do some of that mustard seed math on earth right now—today—through each of us. Our role in this period of history—between when Jesus rose from the dead and when He returns—is to give God space to operate in our individual lives.

Someone asked me recently, "What is your purpose in life?" As a direct result of writing this book, I said, "To make more room for God."

"What do you mean?" asked my friend.

"I mean that at the end of each day there is more room for God in my heart than there was the day before," I answered. "It means that at the end of each day there is more room for God in my home and marriage than there was the day before. It means that when I move out of our neighborhood there is more of Him evident than there was when I moved in."

Have you been viewing yourself as a space maker? Have you been making room for God? Have you been inviting His kingdom and mustard seed math into your life? Have you been inviting His will into your life, or are you insisting on your will instead?

How does a person make room for God? First and foremost, he or she does so by keeping a clean heart and growing to maturity, topics which are discussed in detail in the next section of the book (Part Four – Process: How Do We Live With a Clean Heart?). Once consistent personal growth is established, there is both an offensive and defensive approach to being a light for Christ. For maximum impact, these two approaches operate in tandem.

Just this morning, the girls and I were watching the movie, *Miracle*, about the 1980 US Men's Hockey team that stunned the world and won the gold medal in the 1980 Olympics. As Caitlin and I were watching, we commented that it would be hard to pick the MVP for the game. Mark Johnson scored two out of the three goals for the 3–2 win. Jim Craig made forty-three saves to keep the Russian puck out of the net. Who gets commended most for the win, the defensive or offensive efforts of the American team? The truth is that one without the other would have resulted in a lost game. Both kinds of lights are needed to win the game.

Offensive strategy #1: Invite

Invite God into everything you do. I boldly say to God in prayer on a consistent basis that He is invited into my neighborhood, my property, and my home. Every year my kids enter a new school, I encircle the school in prayer while driving or walking. It's my way of dedicating that spot on earth to God—I call it my "dirt." I invite Him into the space where my children spend most of their time. I invite God to reveal His glory in and through the students. I fully believe every day our children's school day ends, there is more room for God in their school than there was the previous day. Perhaps a teacher is getting closer to knowing Him. Perhaps a student made a decision to trust Christ. Perhaps another student is maturing spiritually through trials. Maybe someone is attracted to the character of Christ as seen in one of my children. I don't know the specifics of what God is doing, but He gets elbow room every time someone dares to give Him space to operate if He wants to—and He always wants to! Right now, there are things happening in my neighborhood and kids' schools that don't involve me at all, but they may be occurring because at least one woman—that would be me—has unabashedly invited God to operate and show His glory. Invite Him into your problems, your marriage, your friendships, and your decision-making. Let Him know every day and in everything, "God, I want Your story!" We are to be praying for God's will in heaven to be occurring here on earth (Matthew 6:10).

Offensive strategy #2: Initiate

Once we invite God into a circumstance involving others, for example, we must take the initiative to make room for Him. We can do this by bringing up His name or creating an environment where relationships can be developed for His purposes. God will rush in and do something great, which may or may not be evident at the time. The number of ideas to make room for God is endless and can be worked out personally between you and God based on your gifts, talents, and schedule. Some examples from my life follow. I have conducted weekly Bible studies in my home. I have hosted community events so neighbors know the way to our house just in case God wants to use us in their lives. I have forged friendships with some neighbors that will last a lifetime. Any decision you make that creates space for Jesus to operate counts as an offensive move for the kingdom of God.

Offensive strategy #3: Invest

Hang in there for a while in relationships. Allow some depth to develop between you and others around you. Don't just invite or initiate once then quit because God didn't seem to do anything. Don't just think, "That person is now checked off my list." Don't let the door close on any relationship in your life, whether you see the person once a year or once a week.

An athlete with an offensive role on any team waits for any and all opportunities to score. In soccer, the opportunity may not come until the last ten minutes of the ninety-minute game. In order to be able to seize the opportunity to score late in the game when fatigue has set in, a player must still be found vigilant. It's the same with relationships with people. Thinking offensively means being open to all opportunities and keeping all opportunities open (Colossians 4:5–6). For example, my stepchildren come in and out of my life. I let them. I don't want to force myself on them, but I shut no doors. All doors are open today as I type. I haven't seen a few of them for a while, but I am not going anywhere, whether they enter back into a relationship with us a few weeks from now, a few years, or a few decades.

The offensive part of being a light for Jesus is to invite, initiate, and invest in people. It takes energy, purpose, and deliberate decisions to be outgoing. For some of you, being offensive is right up your alley. For others, being a defensive light will come more naturally.

Defensive strategy #1: Respond well to people

Our daughter, Caitlin, is a student-athlete in college on the women's soccer team. So far, she has played mostly defense. Her role is to keep the opposing side from scoring goals by having good field vision, performing strong tackles, delivering quality passes, and executing winning game strategies with her teammates. It's thrilling to watch her shut down an offensive player when she is playing her position well.

As a Christian, defense means minimizing the opportunity for the opponent (Satan) to score. Satan scores every time he gets more room to operate. He gets that room when he tempts someone and he or she takes the bait. The Christian's job is to cut off Satan's angle and shut him down.

An example of what can happen when we play defense by living according to the Bible can be found in Paul's letter to the Philippians:

> Do everything without complaining or arguing, so that you may become blameless and pure, children of God without fault in a crooked and depraved generation, in which you shine like stars in the universe.
>
> —Philippians 2:14

What would happen if complaining and arguing were erased from our lives? What would happen if we responded well to others? We would be an instant and incredible contrast of light to the dark world around us without even leading a Bible study or hosting an event in our homes. We would simply be responding in a godly manner to the world around us and everyone we know would notice.

> But I tell you: Love your enemies and pray for those who persecute you . . . If you love those who love you, what reward will you get? Are not even the tax collectors doing that? And if you greet only your brothers, what are you doing more than others? Do not even pagans do that?
>
> —Matthew 5:44, 46–47

What would happen if we suddenly treated everyone with love, even the people who are difficult to be around? Sometimes we don't feel warm and fuzzy around those who are harsh or indifferent, but we can extend kindness in spite of what we feel. We can be an instant and incredible light contrasting against the dark world around us.

Defensive strategy #2: Respond well to Satan's strategies

Much of our light for Christ isn't shown so much in what we do offensively, but in how we respond defensively to the shots Satan launches our way. It used to depress me that I couldn't control other human beings. To accept that truth means an instant vulnerability to the harms of life. It means my life can be adversely affected in countless ways by those around me. Grappling with this reality has led me to the tools I now cling to in order to be a good responder, a good defensive player for Jesus. Folks, we can get up each morning with our chins up, our backs straight, and our shoulders squared in confidence because of the following two truths:

1. We have everything we need in Jesus alone.

"For in Christ, all the fullness of deity dwells in bodily form, and you have been given fullness in Christ, who is the head over all power and authority" (Colossians 2:10). This verse is important to get. Read it again. Jesus doesn't *give* us what we need. He *is* what we need. Jesus lives in you through the power of the Holy Spirit. If you need strength, Jesus doesn't give you strength; He *is* strength. If you need courage, He *is* courage. If you need wisdom, He *is* wisdom. If you need love, He *is* love.

When my feelings tell me otherwise, I can be found in places like the laundry room saying aloud, "Lord, I thank You that I have everything I need in You alone. I do not need my family members to cooperate with me, and I don't need a day off. Otherwise, You would be giving those to me. Holy Spirit, respond *for* me because I am tired and angry. Override my tired body, frazzled mind, and strained emotions so the world gets to see You instead of me."

On days when the rest of the world isn't cooperating with me, I love the promise of 2 Corinthians 9:8: "And God is able to make *all* grace abound to you, so that in *all* things at *all* times, having *all* that you need, you will abound in *every* good work" [emphasis added]. The all-inclusive language in this verse covers every situation I face and everything I need to do. Amazing.

The truth that I have everything I need in Jesus alone provides me with peace as I rise to face each day. The next truth protects me from feeling like a victim to whatever is transpiring around me.

2. No one can take away our power to respond.

I have come to understand that no one can mess up God's story for me unless I allow it. Someone may speak cruelly to me, but I don't have to respond back in anger and dim my light for God. Someone may let me down, but I can still respond in forgiveness.

People will notice a difference in us if we do nothing else but respond well to the world around us. If we love those who are not easy to love, we will look different from others who only love those who love them back. When you and I respond well, it's like each of us becomes a movie screen that gives everyone who knows us the opportunity to view something else . . . something different . . . something bright. Since God is telling the story, our reaction will have impact. He will rush in and fill the space we give Him by stopping the shot Satan is trying to score.

I can trust that when I respond well to the chaos around me, I shine like a star in the universe in God's story. So, I aim high. I strive to pay attention and respond well all day long to each sentence exchanged between others and me. There are no circumstances that grant a loophole or excuse a poor response. After all, my Savior was crucified and never sinned. So even in conflict, when overwhelmed with stress, and when poorly treated, I pray I exemplify Philippians 1:27: "Whatever happens, conduct yourselves in a manner worthy of the gospel of Christ."

Do you want to shine brightly but don't know where to start or what to do? Just start by responding well to those around you . . . The co-worker who bugs you, the roommate who never puts things away, the neighbor who ignores you, the spouse who says cruel words, the boyfriend who lets you down, and the friend who breaks a promise. You will shine like a star in the universe and people around you will learn what it means to receive God's brand of love.

Life is filled with opportunities for us to be space makers and to make room for God. We can respond to difficult circumstances offensively when we invite, initiate, and invest. In prayer, we invite God into everything we do. We *initiate* by creating opportunities for people to engage in spiritual discussions. We *invest* in people. Sometimes that means we remain in hard relationships because God is asking us to stay long and to love lavishly. As space makers, we can also use the defensive strategy of responding well to difficult people. Our confidence rests in the truths that *we have everything we need in Jesus alone*, and *no one can take away our power to respond* in a way that makes room for God to work.

What would the world look like if we would all make room for God to operate everywhere we go? We would light up the globe.

Chapter Ten

Is Our Perspective ABOVE the Chaos or IN It?

We have just been contemplating a variety of metaphors for viewing ourselves through God's eyes and seeing how we can light up our dark world for Christ. Has this material caused you to see yourself differently? Do you hear God calling, "Where are you?" He wants you to join His eternal story. Were you inspired to be a firework, a picture frame, a mathematician, a soldier, or a space maker?

Why is it important to view ourselves through God's eyes? We all know that the way we view ourselves impacts how we choose to live our lives. When I get out of bed in the morning with God's perspective on the forefront of my mind, I seize opportunities to discuss spiritual matters in my conversations. When I spend my days with an eye toward the string no matter the circumstances, I live ABOVE the chaos around me.

Unfortunately, I have lost perspective on far too many days. When I begin my day thinking first about my job as a teacher, instead of first being a Christian who happens to be a teacher, all I do is teach academic material and go home. When I am first and foremost a mom instead of a Christian who happens to be a mom, I get through the day caring for my children and keeping the house clean, but I may never once bring up God.

I know many of us can forget the value and purpose of our lives in God's eyes and become more concerned with school work, house projects, jobs, and social activities. When God and people are not first, we are not living with a perspective above the chaos; instead, we are living with a perspective *in* the chaos.

At the end of Part Two – Living ABOVE the Chaos, I shared my opinion that the Bible is not receiving enough concerted attention by many Christ followers. I challenged us to consider the uniqueness of the Bible and to invest regularly in getting to know its contents. As we conclude Part Three – Perspective: How Should We View Our Lives?, I ask us to take an honest look at our behavior in order to evaluate how we are doing with perspective. I believe if we are seeing ourselves as God sees us, then we will be living as God asks us to live.

How we act is the litmus test of what we *really* believe and how we *really* see ourselves. If we say we believe people need a Savior, but put no effort into sharing Him, then we *really* don't believe people need a Savior. Some of you would frantically exclaim, "Yes! I do believe people need a Savior! I do!" Well then, produce evidence that you are living as a light for Him. If you are unable to provide proof, I would argue that indicates you don't *really* believe you are God's firework.

If we say we believe God wove us together in our mother's womb, but can't smile at our reflection in the mirror, struggle significantly with body image, and become preoccupied with comparison when in a crowded room, then we don't *really* believe we are God's picture frame. If we say we believe God can accomplish miraculous eternal results with whatever we offer Him, but never take a scary step of faith that gives Him room to show up and do something amazing, then we don't *really* believe we are God's mathematicians. If we say there is evil in the world and yet live carelessly—selecting relationships haphazardly, handling sin in a sloppy manner, and adhering to ideas before comparing them to biblical standards—then we don't *really* believe we are God's soldiers. If we say God has purpose for us in whatever our circumstances and wherever we live, but we keep waiting until we move out of our apartment complex to initiate relationships with neighbors, or waiting until the next job to live transparently as a Christian with co-workers, then we don't *really* believe we are God's space makers.

I am deeply concerned that many of us lack God's perspective of our lives. As a result, we are living carefully, predictably—and invisibly. We are living largely for the dot, not the string. I believe if we could see ourselves through lenses—such as the ones I have presented in this "Perspective" section—that we would understand the critical and unified role we play on earth and would daily *live out* all that the Bible says we are. The world wouldn't know what to do with us. We wouldn't be invisible anymore!

On most days, I feel lonely as a Christian, and I don't believe it's because there aren't many of us around. Be not fooled, there are many of us! Just attend a Beth Moore *Living Proof* conference or a *Passion* conference of college students packed in cavernous spaces like the Georgia Dome! It's in places like that we can look around and *know* we are not alone. In fact, we are a huge army with representatives around the entire world.

I believe the reason it *feels* like so few Christians are around is because we are weak on perspective. I believe Christians *seem* scarce because so many of us are hiding our lights "under a basket" and keeping our faith a secret. We do this for numerous reasons.

Perhaps some of us have chosen not to live transparently as believers because our lifestyles don't look any different than the lifestyles of those who don't yet know Christ. We call ourselves Christians, but are not Christ followers. We tolerate sin in our lives because we don't have God's perspective about our role as picture frames for reflecting both God's love and holiness, for instance.

A few weeks ago, I was visiting a church where a guest speaker shared the story of the woman caught in adultery and brought to Jesus in front of a group. Jesus said to her accusers, "If any of you is without sin, let him be the first to throw a stone at her" (John 8:7). The crowd dispersed until only the woman and Jesus were left alone together.

The speaker then left the storyline and encouraged members of the church to love all people no matter the color of their skin or the number of tattoos or piercings on their bodies. I left disturbed—not about loving all kinds of people—I do! I was bothered because the speaker never finished the story. Christ's last words to the woman as they stood alone were, "Go now and leave your life of sin" (John 8:11). Is it my imagination, or has the pendulum swung toward God's love at the exclusion of His holiness? As a result, it feels to me that sin is largely being left unaddressed in a widespread manner among Christians and churchgoers.

I know people who attend church every Sunday but cannot forgive an offense. Some Christian parents lie to the school by saying their children are sick when they are not. I notice students from private Christian schools using a voracious amount of profanity.

Speaking of profanity, I also notice an increasing number of Christians "soft swearing" as part of normal conversation. I'm sure you know what substitute words cross my mind when I hear "freakin," "crap," "dang," or "What the. . ." There is the argument that "We aren't as bad as the people around us using the real words," but can we hang the banner of the name of Jesus over our heads without embarrassment? I am not so sure (Colossians 3:7–8).

Our speech isn't the only issue. There is drinking in excess, misuse of sex, and the practice of acting hypocritically based on who we are with and what we are doing. These seem prevalent in an alarming number of Christian churches and circles. For a seven-year season, they were sadly prevalent in me. Now, when others discover that I am a follower of Christ, I hope they think: *I didn't know that, but I am not surprised at all.* I hope they don't think: *You have got to be kidding! Her?* I would have gotten this latter response during the years I responded poorly to Dan's death. I am saddened by the fact that I did not have a perspective that lifted me above the chaos. There's nothing I can do to go back and relive that time, but I can purpose to never underestimate the importance of perspective again. A relaxed perspective leads to relaxed standards, and keeps me from living transparently as a Christ follower.

Besides tolerating sin, which leads to a lack of transparency, some Christians are afraid of being mocked or ignored if they openly associate with Jesus Christ. This apprehension is fueled by a culture that is increasingly intolerant of any rigid line being drawn—as if embracing diversity denies the existence of or search for truth. Whatever the reasons for not associating our lives with Jesus Christ, too many Christians are prone to blending in instead of lovingly and purely standing out.

One of two crucial elements to maintaining a strong perspective is to know the Bible. Hopefully the information in Chapter Four: Are you living ABOVE the Chaos or IN it? reaffirmed your understanding that the Bible is no ordinary book. It is "God-breathed" and equips us for "every good work" (2 Timothy 3:16–17). God uses it to change us. Find a way to read, study, and discuss the Bible on a consistent basis. It's our greatest mode of safety against erroneous thinking that can lead to a lack of perspective.

Personally, I get nervous when I am not turning the pages of my Bible on a regular basis. I also find that if I am not enjoying the Bible with a small group of people, I am prone to slip into *reading* the Bible instead of *delighting* in it. Quite honestly, too, I don't learn as much when I am alone! Meeting regularly with a group of Christ followers to study the Bible will keep our involvement with God's Word consistent.

We should be careful about the groups we join, however. Let's meet together with people who understand the basic framework of God's story so discussions don't get bogged down in swapping opinions without examining matters in light of what the Bible says. Hebrews 10:25 tells us: "Let us not give up meeting together, as some are in the habit of doing, but let us encourage one another—and all the more as you see the Day approaching."

In addition to the study of the Bible, prayer plays a crucial role in maintaining God's perspective about our lives. I began this chapter by explaining I can get out of bed in the morning seeing myself as a Christ follower first and foremost and then live for the string; or I can get out of bed with a weak perspective and then dot activities dominate my thinking. Prayer is also a deciding factor in which way my day goes. When I don't pray, I get sucked into the dot and lose touch with God and people. When I do pray, I see opportunities to live for the string everywhere I turn.

When I pray, my eyes are lifted to the face of my Father and my perspective is realigned. As I communicate concerns about dot activities, I remember the string and eternal matters are more important. As I consider relationships, I remember souls. When tempted to think I am responsible for producing particular results, I remember Who is in charge. When I speak about feelings of loneliness and disappointment, I remember that I am loved, special, significant, and never alone. Prayer keeps me connected to the larger story happening around me. I can say with the psalmist David, "I lift up my eyes to the hills—where does my help come from? My help comes from the Lord, the Maker of heaven and earth" (Psalm 121:1).

Oh, how I hope you have been reminded about the crucial role perspective plays in living a life that displays strength and beauty no matter what. Perspective fuels the desire to adjust our actions so we represent Christ well. However, we also need to understand that our hearts need to change too. And change is a process brought about as we cooperate with the Holy Spirit in our lives. In Part Four – Process: How Do We Live With a Clean Heart?, we will begin to unpack the secrets of how God gains room to display Himself through us so that collectively we light up the world.

Part Four

Process: How Do We Live With a Clean Heart?

Chapter Eleven

Beginning the Process of Living with a Clean Heart

> Is God getting His way with me, and are other people beginning to see God in my life more and more?
>
> —Oswald Chambers[1]

What would people who have known you for a long time say about your growth as a person over the span of years? Would they say (1) you are exactly the same as you have always been, (2) you have digressed in character, or (3) you have become more Christ-like with every year? I personally know people in each of the three categories, and I am committed to living my life in such a way that people say, "She is becoming more Christ-like with each passing year." I want to have a clean heart and be increasing in my ability to shine brightly.

Now that our eyes can better see God's magnificent, overarching, safe, loving plan—now that we have perspective—we need to address matters of the heart in order to live ABOVE the chaos. Entering into the process of growth in the Christian life will allow us to venture even further into the richness of His story for each of us.

I have already explained one of the two major reasons I did not make it through the tragedy of Dan's death. First, I did not understand the battle strategies of the enemy, and therefore, was ill-equipped to recognize or combat the lies that came my way. This chapter begins to address the *second* reason I did not endure Dan's death well. My heart was not clean.

You may know the illustration about the duck that appears to be serenely floating on the water's surface, but underneath is paddling like crazy. Well, from the outside my early Christian life looked accomplished, but underneath my heart was messy. When I thought about pleasing God with my life, I believed behavior trumped the condition of my heart. After all, I reasoned, behavior is what people see, so that counts more. I had the Christian life collapsed into a checklist of things like reading my Bible, leading Bible studies, and being involved in Christian organizations. My activities were admirable, but because they were disconnected from the condition of my heart, I never operated from deep within myself. My spiritual roots were *truly* only skin deep.

My erroneous thinking caused me to judge people. If someone's life didn't look "in order," I assumed they were doing poorly with God. Or, if I didn't see observable changes for the better in a person, I thought that meant something was going wrong. I viewed people according to their behavior only, and never thought to have greater concern for people's hearts instead. I had a lot to learn.

Living the Christian life involves commitment to a process. It means day-by-day hard work and ruthless determination to pay attention to the heart. If you dare to live with a clean heart, you get to experience the unbelievable reward of turning around sometime in your future and seeing that you are a different person—you look more like Christ than you used to, and you love who you are becoming!

Below I share some of what I have learned about growth as it relates to living with a clean heart. To begin with, I didn't understand that the process of living with a clean heart involves the removal of layers from our lives.

The concept of layers

Imagine that each stack of books in this diagram represents an individual, and each book represents the imperfections in a person's mind, heart, and behavior on the day he or she comes to know Christ as Savior. Each book, each imperfection, is a layer. The layers are unique for each individual on earth. Not only do people have different numbers of layers, the layers also differ in thickness, order, labeling, and the amounts of adhesion between them. No two people are alike.

When we place our faith in Christ, there are new things that become true of us. The Holy Spirit comes to live inside of us (Romans 8:9) and gifts us with many blessings. These include: adoption into the family of God (Ephesians 1:5); forgiveness of our sins (Romans 8:1); assurance of eternal life (John 3:16); and sanctification—being set apart for God's purposes (1 Corinthians 1:2; 2 Thessalonians 2:13). Rarely, however, are any of these inward realities immediately visible. To those who know us best, we still look the same as we did the day before we trusted in Christ. It takes time to establish new habits, reform language, transform thinking, and change habitual reactions that do not honor God. None of the sinful layers have been removed yet. Change involves a process. Change is also good.

> And we know that in all things God works for the good of those who love him, who have been called according to his purpose. For those God foreknew he also predestined to be conformed to the likeness of his Son, that he might be the firstborn among many brothers.
>
> —Romans 8:28–29

God's goal with our lives is not to ensure our comfort, but to conform us to the image of His Son. Layer by layer—or book by book—the Holy Spirit begins to move through our hearts, taking one cleansing swipe after another. Gradually, we begin to look more like Jesus because more of Jesus shines through, as seen in the diagram on the left.

J
E
S
U

I think of this transformational process every autumn. As summer gives way to fall, chlorophyll in leaves gives way to the glorious colors underneath and sets landscapes ablaze. In much the same way, as our layers give way to the Holy Spirit's control over areas of our lives, Christ can be seen through us in all His blazing glory.

How a layer is exposed

In order to address any given problem in our lives, we must first *see* the problem. God uses natural consequences to help us identify many of our imperfections. When we get caught in a lie, we suffer relational fallout. When a person gets a DUI citation, he or she pays a fine, goes to jail, or gets his or her license revoked. When we don't study, we get poor grades. When we mismanage money our checks bounce or our credit card debt increases. Each of these natural occurrences puts us in a position to address the issues head-on without God ever having to "punish" us. When we suffer the natural consequences of our behavior, God is making us better. By allowing us to see the bad stuff, He gives us an opportunity to get mad at it, get rid of it, and in turn to reflect more of the good stuff, the Person of Jesus Christ.

> My son, do not make light of the Lord's discipline, and do not lose heart when he rebukes you, because the Lord disciplines those he loves, and he punishes everyone he accepts as a son.
>
> —Hebrews 12:5

My father is a contractor who restores old homes. When he begins a new project, the first thing he does is tear down parts of the home, or he may gut it completely. When he drives away at the end of the first day, the home looks worse as a consequence, but progress has been made! Making a mess is not always bad news.

When God messes up our lives a bit to expose the layers that need to be dealt with, there is progress, not digression. I cried when I found out I was pregnant and realized that my secret dating activities would be exposed for the world to see. But, I will always point to that Easter Sunday in the bathtub as the actual hand of God operating as a jackhammer to lift the layer of game-playing and secret-keeping out of my life! Once my behavior was exposed, Satan lost a lot of ground in his battle to keep me ignorant, weak, and ineffective for God.

Sometimes a layer in our lives is exposed privately instead of publicly. For example, many of your thoughts and motives are only known by God and you. He can convict you about improper thoughts toward a friend—perhaps you are focusing on appearance instead of the heart. Another example is only God and you know when you are putting on a façade. He can reveal one night while you are driving home from an event that you were a fake the entire evening. Matters such as these can be dealt with through heartfelt prayers and confession without anyone else ever knowing.

By way of review, I present two truths above regarding my understanding of how to have a clean heart and how to grow. The first is that living with a clean heart involves a growth process whereby God removes layers. The second is that God exposes layers through natural consequences and private revelation. In the remainder of this chapter, I will discuss two more lessons I have learned: we cannot trust that we know what God is up to in the hearts of others; and we are co-laborers with God in removing layers from our lives.

How little we know

When my children and I are in the car, we play a guessing game to deal with the behavior of other drivers. If someone passes us at an insane speed, we say things like, "Maybe his wife is having a baby, and she just called to say she is at the hospital in labor." If someone is in front of us at a stop sign, and seems to be day-dreaming, and misses her turn to pull out, we say things like, "Maybe her mom just died, and she is returning from the funeral and is deep in thought." When we play this game (sometimes laughing at the hilarious things we come up with), we acknowledge that we don't *know*. We are looking at the visible behavior, the top layer; but we really have no right to assume we understand the behavior since we do not *know* what is driving the behavior.

But what about people we have known for a long time, you might ask? This coming summer, I will have been married for twenty-two years. My husband knows me very well, but he does not yet understand me completely. Further, he was not with me every minute of every day of the thirty-two years I lived before we met. He is qualified to make guesses, but he is not qualified to *know*. The same is true of me toward him. Neither of us is God, who knows everything.

Prior to adopting our son when he was two and a half, we were his legal guardians for one year. The day after this sweet toddler first arrived in our home, I took him to the grocery store. He was fussy and could not be comforted. I felt the condescending stares of other people. You know the kind. *Why can't you control your kid, lady?* I was tempted to say, "I just met him yesterday! We don't know each other yet!"

I went to my car deep in thought. I felt convicted. I have glared at parents of misbehaving kids. Until that day, however, it never crossed my mind that perhaps it was the child's first day in a new family. The point is, people know nothing. I *know* nothing.

Understanding that people are layered and that I do not have insight into their layers, keeps me from judging them. These understandings have been life-changing. When I am really puzzled, I just think: *If I could have seen that person's life leading up to today, I would be able to understand what I am seeing.* Better yet: *If I had that person's genetics and exact life experience, I would be just like him or her.* Both of these perspectives assist me greatly in minimizing any air of arrogance or judgment. They also help me to comprehend the kind of growth that is needed to live with a clean heart, and to live ABOVE the chaos.

By now, this may seem like an obvious statement, but we cannot trust our perceptions of what is internally driving external behaviors. Glance back a few pages at the diagram of stacked books within "The concept of layers" section. When we see a *visible* layer in someone that needs to come off—like drug addiction—we don't know if another *unseen* layer has to come off first—like insecurity. As noted earlier, we also never know the thickness of a given layer, what strength or time is needed to lift it off, or just how integrated that layer is in another's life.

Let's say you know someone who uses profanity unabashedly on a regular basis. You watch her brash language erode relationships, ruin job opportunities, and create confusion when people hear she attends church. Caring about her, you address the issue. Very lovingly, you talk to her repeatedly about the damage her profanity is causing. What you don't know, however—and she may not know either—is she suffers from anxiety in relationships caused by being abandoned and rejected in her childhood. Profanity keeps people at bay, which is how she likes it. In her mind, better to have social skills chase people away than people leaving when they discover she is unlovable. Using crass language is a Band-Aid to her anxiety about relationships. Swearing makes her feel powerful and in control. She knows her persona is a fake, but it's the best she can do today until God heals wounds below the surface that are not observable to others.

I was in the parking lot at work recently when I heard a horn being blared in aggravation. I looked up to see a driver honking angrily because a car in front of her would not proceed through a stop sign. I had a side view of the situation which allowed me to see why the driver at the stop sign had not moved along. Two geese were taking their time crossing the road in front of her. Meanwhile, the driver behind her, who could not see the strolling geese, continued to honk angrily. I stared at that angry person and thought: *You look like an idiot.*

I have been that honking idiot.

I have loudly asked individuals to change their behavior while not being privy to the unseen things that had to be worked out inside them before they could straighten out their behaviors. While I honk loudly about someone's hoarding, for example, God may first be trying to deal with the rejection that's causing him or her to reach for material possessions rather than healthy relationships with people and God. Meanwhile, I am speaking so loudly in the person's ear that I am drowning out God's voice. I am in His way.

Neither you nor I can guess what God intends for the future of any person we know, which renders us unqualified to discern what order of events must take place to unravel the past of any of our friends or family members. *We must set each other free to address issues in the order God determines.* The process is messy, but it doesn't necessarily mean things are going awry. It could be that God is allowing life to get messy in order to expose hidden layers and grow that person—to teach him or her about Him, to mature him or her, or to bring about wholeness.

Previously in this book, I have written about my daughter who was diagnosed with lupus a year before going to college. Over a period of months, her health improved and she was able to enter a university as a student-athlete. But then her life fell apart. She has bravely decided to share in her own words how her freshman year unfolded and how she experienced God's growth process first-hand:

> My mom has spoken about how God allows our lives to unravel in the confines of His love and safety in order to show us parts of our hearts that are blocking Him. I had heard of the process of gaining a clean heart, but had not begun to experience it until last year. Here is my story.
>
> Soccer was always second nature to me. I had high hopes of going far with my soccer career. When I was diagnosed with Systemic Lupus in high school, the hopeful future I had envisioned for myself was suddenly jeopardized. After a long college search with many setbacks and struggles, I still managed to arrive at a Division I school as a student-athlete. My hopes for success in soccer were revived. Within weeks of arriving, however, I became ineligible to play as a result of a back injury. In addition, my blood test results skyrocketed, indicating that my lupus was active. Far from home, I began new medications with scary side effects. My life was out of control. I couldn't control my injury, my playing time, or my health. But there was one thing I found that I had complete control over, and that was my food intake. I exchanged soccer disappointments and poor health for body image and appearance; I was thinking this would make me happy. After

completing only one semester of college, I returned home and entered rehab for an eating disorder.

I couldn't understand why all of these negative things would present themselves at such a crucial time in my life. I was constantly asking, "When will God do something good in my life?" I now see some of the re-construction He has been undertaking in my heart. Because God loves me, He has taken away the things I had always trusted in to make me feel good about myself. My lonely pit of darkness in college is what prepared my heart for God and His truth to shine into my life for the first time.

I returned back to my parent's home with an open heart to accept His guidance and plans for my life. Honestly, I began to take my relationship with God seriously for the first time. In addition, I have established a closer relationship with my mom. After nineteen years of letting her advice go in one ear and out the other, I find myself now striving to look more and more like her every day. But one of the most important understandings I have gained through the past six months is that spiritual battle exists. I am learning not to let Satan gain a foothold in my thoughts, but to have my mind constantly filled instead with God's truth about who I am in Christ. I am beautiful in Christ. My relationship with God has grown drastically since coming home.

I am starting to experience what my mom talks about. Chaos exists around us and even *in* us, but when we let God grow us through our circumstances, we rise above the chaos by growing more

> strong and beautiful no matter what. I haven't suffered like Job, but after all his suffering ended, I have an idea of what he meant when he said, "My ears had heard of you, but now my eyes have seen you" (Job 42:5). What I have suffered is worth what I've gained—more of God.

I don't know what people are thinking about my sweet daughter or our family as they watch us suffer. My daughter's story reminds me that none of us are qualified to make accurate assessments about what is going on in the heart of another person or family. *In the same way there are Christians who look great on the outside but aren't doing so great in their hearts (like I was before Dan died), and there are Christians who don't look so good on the outside, but their hearts are on a healthy path of growth (like my daughter when she was in rehab).*

Beware of expecting people to tackle layers in their lives based on what *you* can see and according to *your* growth schedule and order. We must trust that God is unraveling what blocks Christ, even when God's efforts are not visible to us. This perspective will prevent us from speaking too loudly, frequently, or carelessly. None of us wants to be a honking idiot.

How we co-labor

Since only God knows what is needed to grow a person, does that mean we don't lovingly confront people when we see problems such as addiction, dishonesty, fear, hypocrisy, and laziness? Of course we must speak! We co-labor with God as He grows us and as He grows others. He may reveal to us that another person has a problem, and He may call us to participate with Him in helping that person. God leads and we join Him with our part: loving, teaching, encouraging, and speaking the truth. Whenever we address a layer we see in another person, we must do so humbly and gently since God will also be working on a layer in us as we speak. Galatians 6:1 says, "Brothers, if someone is caught in sin, you who are spiritual should restore him gently. Watch yourself, or you also may be tempted."

There is no room for haughty tones and arrogant stances when one layered Christ-follower interacts with any other layered individual. If we let God tackle the layers in others, while we pray and provide supportive communication as needed—slowly and surely that person will become more like Jesus. And we will become more like Jesus also.

By understanding the concept of layers, we have a better idea of what we can and cannot control in our lives and in the lives of others. We can trust God with the order and manner in which the layers are dealt with in ourselves and others. Understanding layers helps us be more compassionate and less judgmental of others which can only help our relationships and help us be a bright light for Him.

This realization that people are layered marked the beginning of my journey in understanding how God grows us. When God points out a layer, we should promptly participate with the Master Contractor as He chips away at the exposed mess. This accelerates the lifting off of layers and allows us to grow more quickly. I am learning that circumstances don't have to veer any of us off the path of steady, consistent growth in our relationships with God. The process of growing year-by-year instead of stagnating or digressing isn't out of my control, or yours. As a result of these understandings, we should no longer see ourselves as victims of haphazard circumstances, but rather as co-managers in a growth process that will result in a clean heart. God invites us to partner with Him in our growth.

Prior to ending this chapter, I want to make one clarification regarding the ways in which the Holy Spirit works in us and with us to produce growth. First, when we partner with the Holy Spirit in our growth, it is by our responses only. For example, the Holy Spirit conceived Jesus within Mary. She did not initiate, plan, or ask for that to occur. She responded by partnering with the Spirit and seeing the pregnancy through, but she could not take credit for the development of the miraculous child within her womb. When Jesus was born, He was the work of the Holy Spirit.

In addition, sometimes the Holy Spirit surprises us in the way He works by addressing a layer we don't expect Him to address. He may also transform us in ways we would not select for ourselves. Or maybe He will call us to duties we cannot imagine completing. We co-labor only in our responses to His workings, but we initiate none of His work, accomplish none of the transformation, and in the end, He alone must get the glory for the result. In the next three chapters, we will look more closely at the ways in which we partner with the Holy Spirit to see growth take place in our lives.

Chapter Twelve

Inviting the Holy Spirit to Take Over Our Hearts

In the next three chapters of Part Four – Process: How Do We Live with a Clean Heart?, I will present three components of experiencing optimum growth, all of which explore the role of the Holy Spirit in our lives and our responses to His leadings. The components are:

- Inviting the Holy Spirit to take over our hearts.
- Confessing everything God shows us.
- Doing everything we know to do.

The first two components are accomplished through prayer, and the last through obedience. When applied together, these components produce consistent growth—even in the toughest circumstances.

These components require hard work, but here is the good news! As you give God His rightful place in every area of your life, He will shine through you more each year. People who know you will recognize that something transformational is occurring, and that it's God getting more room in you. Mustard seed math occurs everywhere you look when God has your heart. This is because He is set free to shine for Who He is.

Each child of God has the Holy Spirit inside of him or her (Romans 8:9). However, the Holy Spirit can be resisted (Acts 7:51). We cannot assume the Holy Spirit will barge into our messy hearts and fill us up when not invited. But when He is invited, He comes (Luke 11:13) and produces change (2 Thessalonians 2:13). Therefore, in order to see transformation in our lives, we must ask the Holy Spirit to take over our hearts.

Before one invites the Holy Spirit to take over his or her heart, it makes sense to first understand how He operates and what He expects from us. Think of the trust exercise often utilized in team-building activities. Someone is blind-folded and then asked to free-fall back into another person's arms as a demonstration of complete trust in the person doing the catching. I suspect you need to know what the Holy Spirit is going to do with you before being willing to free-fall into His arms and let Him take over your heart.

Information about the Holy Spirit must be presented carefully and biblically because there are many connotations of the word "spirit." The next two sections, "What the Spirit does with our hearts" and "What the Spirit requires of us," are presented in a somewhat academic manner. Please approach the material like a student studying for an A on a test so that your understanding of the Spirit becomes carefully connected with the teaching of the Bible. I am praying that after you complete your reading, you will have the confidence to invite the Spirit to take over your heart.

What the Spirit does with our hearts

To become like Christ, the Spirit must be at work in us, and we must cooperate with that work. As layers are removed from our lives, the Holy Spirit is able to more freely operate. Let's consider the following analogy. Our hearts are a car and the Person of the Holy Spirit is a constant occupant. At any moment in time, we determine whether the Spirit sits in the passenger seat (while we run our lives) or the driver's seat (while He runs our lives). As each layer is removed from our hearts, the Holy Spirit automatically gets more driving time because of our cooperation in getting rid of the layers. The evidence of our increased cooperation with the Spirit is seen in our changing attitudes and behaviors.

In the following verses we see that God requires us to rid ourselves of certain attitudes and behaviors, and to adopt new ones.

> And do not grieve the Holy Spirit of God, with whom you were sealed for the day of redemption. Get rid of all bitterness, rage and anger, brawling and slander, along with every form of malice. Be kind and compassionate to one another, forgiving each other, just as in Christ God forgave you.
>
> —Ephesians 4:30–32

These verses help me to see that if I want the Holy Spirit to take over my heart, I must confess that I practice the kinds of sins listed, and I must instead practice acts of kindness, compassion, and forgiveness. I need to allow the Holy Spirit to take over the dark places—the layers—so I can do the right kinds of things, and so I can have a clean heart.

When a person accepts Christ as Savior and Lord, the Holy Spirit comes to reside inside him or her for the remainder of his or her life (Romans 8:9). The Holy Spirit's presence in our lives seals us for the day of redemption, when Christ returns again. This idea is born out in 2 Corinthians 1:21–22:

> Now it is God who makes both us and you stand firm in Christ. He anointed us, set his seal of ownership on us, and put his Spirit in our hearts as a deposit, guaranteeing what is to come.

I recently sealed an envelope with a wax impression. It felt very official. The seal bears witness to the authenticity and authority of what is written inside. When God looks at us, He sees His Spirit, and the Spirit of God keeps us sealed for the day of redemption. We cannot lose our salvation. The *ESV Study Bible* explains, "God pours out the Holy Spirit on all of his children to guarantee (or to provide a "down payment" on) their share in his eternal kingdom . . . until we acquire possession of it" (Ephesians 1:13–14).[1]

I liken this idea of sealing to my relationship with my children. When they became members of our family, they became O'Connors. They are sealed in that state as O'Connors. Nothing can change that fact. Besides the Spirit keeping us sealed for salvation, the idea of sealing is related to another amazing blessing God gifts us with when we become believers. It is called sanctification.

Since sanctification is true of all Christians, it is imperative we understand its meaning and purpose. I leaned on the expertise of a seminary graduate, LeAnn, to clarify the two meanings of sanctification, and to present this theological understanding succinctly, which she does here.

There are two main concepts that we need to understand about sanctification. First, sanctification becomes a state of being for the Christian at the time he or she commits his or her life to Christ. Second, God calls believers to become more sanctified throughout the course of their lives. Let's flesh out these concepts using information from *Vine's Complete Expository Dictionary of Old and New Testament Words.*[2]

When we accept Christ as our Savior and commit our lives to Him, the Holy Spirit sanctifies us to God (1 Corinthians 1:2; 2 Thessalonians 2:13). We enter into a state of sanctification. According to *Vine*'s, "to sanctify" something (or someone) is "to set it apart" or "to separate it out" from other things.[3] *Vine's* tells us that those who are sanctified in Jesus are often designated in New Testament Greek as *hagios* which translated into English means "holy ones" or "saints" (see Acts 9:32, 41).[4] Literally, we are made saints—holy ones—by God. Laurie's example above is imperfect, but this "separation" spoken about here is similar to the idea of her children being set apart as O'Connors.

But we have a responsibility to fulfill because we are sealed and sanctified. If we do not fulfill this responsibility, we will not shine like bright lights who can lead others to Christ. This is where the second meaning of sanctification comes in. *Vine's* defines it as "the course of life befitting those so separated."[5] And: "Sanctification is also used in the NT [New Testament] of the separation of the believer from evil things and ways."[6] Because we

> have the Holy Spirit within us, we are to live as if we *are* holy ones set apart for God's purposes.[7]

Returning to my analogy, because each of my children is an O'Connor, each bears the responsibility of going out into the world and acting in a way befitting an O'Connor. Over the years, they have heard me say things like, "O'Connors are kind," "O'Connors make the world a better place," or "O'Connors love Jesus."

Romans 12:1 tells us plainly that because God has been merciful to us, we are to "offer our bodies as living sacrifices, holy and pleasing to God—this is your spiritual act of worship." In other words, we are to use all of our bodily capacities to live holy lives. Throughout our Christian lives we are to enter into a process of growth whereby we let God have more and more of our lives. We do this by inviting the Holy Spirit to take over our hearts and by allowing Him to deal with the layers so Jesus can shine through.

What the Spirit requires of us

There are some more basics we need to understand about the work of the Holy Spirit before we discuss what it means for Him to "take over our hearts." Let's start with the ideas of indwelling and filling. The Spirit *indwells* every Christian (John 14:16–17; Romans 8:9), but not every Christian is *filled*, which means to be controlled by the Spirit (Ephesians 5:18).[8] Recall my simplistic analogy that the Holy Spirit is always present in the car (indwells the heart), but not always in the driver's seat (filling the heart). Our goal is to have the Holy Spirit managing every aspect of our hearts. He should be in the driver's seat all of the time.

In 2 Corinthians we learn that, "As the Spirit of the Lord works within us, we become more and more like him and reflect His glory even more" (3:18). How is the process of becoming more like Him accomplished? It starts with ridding our hearts of sin. The Holy Spirit helps us with that too. Thankfully, we learn in John 16:7–13 that He was sent to guide us into all truth, which includes identifying sin and empowering us to live in truth.

Though the Holy Spirit is the third person of the Godhead and equal to God, I like to think of Him as the energy of God.[9] He is the One Who moves throughout our insides and incites the changes in our hearts that will eventually change our behaviors. In this slow and steady process of growth, the Holy Spirit helps us in many ways. He teaches (John 14:26), guides (Romans 8:14), commands (Acts 8:29), restrains (Genesis 6:3), intercedes (Romans 8:26), and speaks (John 15:26; 2 Peter 1:21).[10] He also inspires (2 Peter 1:21), convinces (John 16:8), and regenerates (John 3:5–6).[11]

Just like God, the Spirit can be obeyed (Acts 10:19–21)—and also resisted (Acts 7:51). The Holy Spirit constantly moves us towards obedience, but it is possible for us to ignore His tapping at the layers that need to be exposed and removed, and hold onto them for dear life. When we resist Him like that, we will suffer the natural consequences of continuing the behaviors and holding onto the heart attitudes we refuse to change. As mentioned, if we don't study for exams, our grades will be lower. If we speed, we will eventually get ticketed. If we lie, we will erode our relationships. If we don't eat well and exercise, we will harm our bodies. If we are prideful, we will suffer disgrace (Proverbs 11:2, 16:18, 29:23). If we judge, we will be judged in return (Matthew 7:1–2).

In addition to suffering consequences, any issue left unchecked will grow and increase its grip on us with each day we refuse to take it captive and address it with God. Eventually, even secret sins become obvious to those who know us best, and we will, most likely, one day be confronted publicly by a family member or friend.

If we don't want to suffer the debilitating consequences of disobedience, we can decide to live as sanctified people in purity and in a way that has us hiding from no one. We can choose to obey, lean hard into what God wants, and allow the Holy Spirit to do His work in us.

And then it happens. Layers come off. They lose their grip. They go away. They thin out. The stack of issues that had been hiding the character of Christ in us gets smaller, and people who know us see more of Jesus with each passing year. Sanctification is occurring. Our set-apartness becomes more evident to others.

I trust that it is God's will that I become sanctified. Therefore, I trust that my perfect God is flawlessly orchestrating circumstances for the next layer to come off. I pay attention. When I see the next area to address, I do so. It's hard, but my obedience takes the layer off. When I turn around later, I am changed. Very changed. Just like an acorn looks nothing like a mature oak tree, so today I look nothing like that twelve-year-old girl who placed her faith in Jesus and made a commitment to follow Him.[12] I also no longer resemble the woman that attended my brother's funeral.

There may be instances where the Holy Spirit chooses to operate in a dramatic fashion. Biblical examples include the Christians who received the Holy Spirit on the day of Pentecost (Acts 2:2–13) and Paul encountering Christ on the road to Damascus (Acts 9:1–21). Most of the time, however, God's work seems to be slow and steady. For any of us to see oak-tree-like change and for growth to occur, we must, through prayer, invite the Holy Spirit to take over our hearts. That's what we will discuss next.

Invite through prayer

Being filled with the Spirit is accompanied by the difficult, life-long task of tackling layers in our lives. Perhaps you are hesitating to throw your heart open to Him in invitation because of this harsh reality, but do so anyway for three critical reasons. First, each of us needs His power.

I am coming to grips with the reality that I can do *nothing* to guarantee a particular result from my actions. I can love someone, but I can't make them love me back. I can apply for a job, but I can't make someone hire me. I can invite guests, but I can't make them come. I can't even guarantee the car will start tomorrow when I turn the key. I am truly powerless except for allowing the Holy Spirit to take over my heart so I am fueled by His power instead of my futile self-effort (John 6:63).

In addition to being fueled by His power, I need His sinless character to replace my flawed one. I am unable to reflect the character of God because God is holy—I am not. I must invite the Holy Spirit to do the job for me. Perhaps most importantly, I want a relationship with the Spirit. Knowing the Spirit creates greater intimacy with the Son and Father as well (John 16:13–15).

These desires for power, character, and relationship are met only through invitation. I want the Holy Spirit to have all the room He needs to boldly invade my life without interruption and show Himself strong through the results He produces from my Spirit-controlled behavior (John 3:34, 7:37–39).

I encourage you to invite the Holy Spirit to take over your heart through prayer. Let God know you want every nook and cranny of your heart to be filled with His Spirit! Because the Spirit is holy, the invitation automatically assumes you have a keen desire to rid your heart of any sin or hindrance that prevents Him from being in the driver's seat. God will certainly point out sins that the Bible speaks to directly, like lying, cheating, and gossip. He will also reveal more subtle interferences that aren't necessarily sin, but might be done in excess or by neglect. These might include spending too much time on social media, too much time at work, and not fully engaging with one's children. Also seeing such softer issues as disruptions to being filled with the Spirit can be tough to admit and address, but learn to embrace the truth even when God reveals more subtle layers. As long as they influence your life, you cannot *fully* reflect the glorious, blameless, creative, ordered, grace-filled character of God to the world around you.

I urge you to do whatever work is needed to set God free within yourself to do as He pleases. It's the only way your life will exhibit God-powered results. It's the only way the world around you will see His character displayed. It is the only way to get to know the God Who created you. Imagine if every Christian invited the Spirit of God to infiltrate every aspect of their life. The world as we know it today would change and we would be bright displays for God indeed!

Invite through lifestyle

Prayer is the first step in inviting the Holy Spirit to take over our lives. After praying, we need to adopt a lifestyle that continually invites the Holy Spirit to be involved in every aspect of our lives. Do we foster friendships with people who are walking with Christ? Have we invited friends like these to speak into our life about things that don't line up with God and His Word? Do we read our Bible consistently so our standards of conduct and attitudes don't slip? Do we read books, watch movies, and listen to music that set our minds on things above?

What about you? Is your entire life an invitation to the Lord? Oftentimes our prayers give a resounding "yes" to that question, but in reality, we do not invite with our lifestyle choices. Use the chart on page 163 to determine how much of an open invitation your life is to the Lord.

If any of the statements in the left-hand column ring true for you, then you have blocks in your life where you are saying, "Lord, You can go here but not there, address this but not that, work in

You find yourself...	You pray...
Saying, "I could never work with her because her personality annoys me."	"Lord, she is difficult, but show me if you want me to be in a relationship with her and I will do it."
Saying, "That is just not an option for me."	"Lord, is that an option for me? If so, I will do it."
Saying, "I won't even consider it."	"Lord, am I to consider that? If so, I will do it."
Saying, "We can't move."	"Lord, are we supposed to move? If so, I will do it."
Ignoring a difficult person by not initiating discussions, e-mails, greetings, and phone calls.	"Lord, show me how to love that person. How can I do it best?"
Ignoring that still, small voice that says you should be addressing something.	"Lord, I invite you into this area and ask you to take over. Show me the steps to take to walk in victory. Talk to me, Lord. I want to hear."

them but not in me." I have a quote from Shelia Walsh in my prayer journal, "Lord, I don't know where You are going today, but I am going with You."[13] This kind of surrendered attitude offers an invitation for the Holy Spirit to take the lead.

A person who invites the Spirit of God into every aspect of his or her life never makes a decision based on circumstances, but according to God's leading—an internal prompting, urging, nudging, or sense of urgency. *The Spirit never leads us to go against the Bible.* God may prompt you to research, collect information, talk with others, or create lists of pros and cons, but never for the purpose of basing a decision on those things. He will employ those things to clear the cobwebs and allow you to recognize His leading.

One of my original sayings is, "You can't figure out God's will sitting on a couch." For me, God's clarity has rarely jumped off the pages of a pro-con list or from a conversation with a friend, even a wise friend of good counsel. My moments of deepest clarity have usually originated during quiet times with God and my Bible. Then I get up to do what I think He is telling me to do. As soon as I start walking out the plan, clarity comes quickly, either as a "Yes, you heard Me correctly, Laurie," or a "Stop, Laurie! That prompting was not from Me."

The Bible tells us: "Whether you turn to the right or to the left, your ears will hear a voice behind you, saying, 'This is the way; walk in it'" (Isaiah 30:21). Sometimes God's leading looks like common sense, logic, or good strategy to those around you, and sometimes it doesn't. For example,

- *As a rule*, I live within a budget and minimize debt. However, there are times I feel led to splurge on an event or person in a way that defies common sense, but I do it because I sense God's leading to do so.

- *As a rule*, I listen for boundary lines in relationships and wisely protect myself from relationships that may be destructive. However, there are times I feel led to befriend someone who is "difficult," and I do it because I sense God's leading to do so.
- *As a rule*, I balance my schedule in order not to become overly committed. However, there are times when I sense God's leading to do something insane, like take on an additional responsibility at work or in the community because of the relationships involved.

In all of these examples, whether in conservative spending or splurging, safety in relationships or risk, balanced schedule or running full-tilt, it's never an issue of what looks good on paper or of adherence to some principle for a happy life. It's always about God's promptings. These can be sensed in a heart that is giving Him as much room to operate as possible by unabashedly inviting Him into all areas of the heart to do as He wishes.

In this chapter, I have talked about taking an active role in our spiritual growth by allowing the Holy Spirit to go anywhere He wishes within us. We then tackle any layers He identifies in order to maintain a clean heart. In light of this process, our circumstances do not hinder the rate at which we grow in our relationship with Christ. *Rather, our circumstances become the means through which the Holy Spirit identifies areas that need to be addressed.* Making room in our hearts for the Holy Spirit is essential if we want to live ABOVE the chaos and display God's strength and beauty. A second component of experiencing optimum growth involves confessing everything God shows us we need to confess. We will discuss this next in Chapter Thirteen.

Chapter Thirteen

Confessing Everything God Shows Us

> Above all else, guard your heart, for it is the wellspring of life.
>
> —Proverbs 4:23

Everything about you—your behavior, words, and attitudes—stems from your heart. In the last chapter, we discussed the first component of fostering consistent growth in our lives no matter what. We need to invite the Holy Spirit to take over our hearts to go anywhere He wishes in order to transform us into a reflection of Himself.

In this chapter, we will talk about how to guard our hearts and keep them clean through understanding a second component for growth: confession. We will learn more specifically how to respond to God and others after the Holy Spirit has revealed sin, so our heart can be the wellspring of life it was created to be (Proverbs 4:23).

It is true that Jesus died for every one of our sins. When we placed our faith in Him, He removed them as far as "the east is from the west" (Psalm 103:12). Once we are Christians, however, it is our job to guard our hearts and keep them pure. We do so through many means—worship, Bible study, prayer, obedience, wise friendship, and productive thinking to name a few. It's this careful work of confession, however, that chips away at the thickest and most stubbornly adhered layers that are blocking Jesus from shining through. Confession increases the space we give God to operate within us. Then, the character of God the Father, God the Son, and God the Holy Spirit can shine more brightly through us. As we enter into this discussion of confession in question and answer format, let's first look at what sin does to our hearts.

Why must we confess our sins?

The reason human beings need to be rescued is because sin has separated us from a holy God. Thankfully, He loved us enough to make a way for us to have a relationship with Him through the death of His Son, Jesus Christ. Though our union with God is established and secure because of Jesus, sin can still interfere in our daily interactions with God. Psalm 66:18 says, "If I had cherished sin in my heart, the Lord would not have listened." An explanation of this verse in the *Treasury of David Commentary* is chilling to me: "If, having seen it to be there, I continue to gaze upon it without aversion; if I cherish, I have a side glance of love toward it, excuse it, and palliate it; the Lord will not hear me."[1]

I certainly have seen sin in my heart without being upset. I have also excused it and have even given it a side glance of love. When I do these things, my relationship with God is affected since I am holding onto something other than Him.

I describe sin to my children as bricks that build walls in our hearts. Every time we sin, it's as if a brick comes and takes up residence, leaving less room for God to move around. If we live a life without confessing sin, those bricks build walls that interfere with our relationships with God and people. We get clogged. It's like when I hurt my husband with my words. He doesn't leave me, but my relationship with him is harmed. The only way to restore the relationship is to confess my wrong doing, to ask for his forgiveness, and to make amends.

It is the same in my relationship with God. In the same way, sincere confession removes bricks in my marriage, heartfelt confession knocks down sin walls and puts God and me on a good path again. Only a life of "confessing as I go" keeps an open relationship with God, leaving the maximum amount of room in my heart for God to move around and to work in and through me.

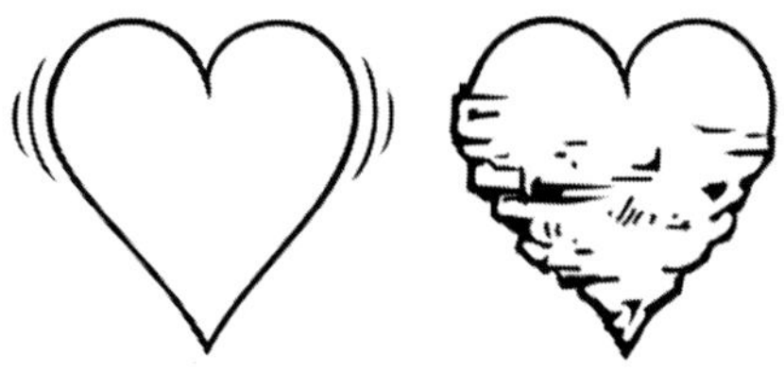

Here is a diagram of what I imagine sin doing to my heart as well as everyone else's. When the bricks disappear, there is an actual sense of weight being lifted off our shoulders and spirits. Life weighs less when we live it clean! It's good news when God shows us sin because we can address it honestly and get rid of it! The psalmist David writes about how miserable he was when he held onto unconfessed sin. While he kept silent about his sin, he felt as if his "bones wasted away" through his constant groaning. He felt God's heavy hand on him day and night, and "his strength was sapped" like "the heat of summer" (Psalm 32:3–4).

I have been there. Haven't you? Guilt makes us miserable. But then David says, ". . . I acknowledged my sin to you and did not cover up my iniquity. I said, 'I will confess my transgressions to the Lord'—and you forgave the guilt of my sin" (Psalm 32:5). I can certainly relate to that kind of relief.

According to 1 John 1:9, "If we confess our sins, he is faithful and just and will forgive us our sins and purify us from all unrighteousness." Confession makes us clean! Don't you want to keep your heart clean—really clean—daily and moment-by-moment? Me too! I have fallen in love with clean! The question now is: How do we confess our sins?

How do we confess our sins?

I referred to 1 John 1:9 above in our discussion as to why we want to confess our sins to the Lord. Let's look more deeply now into how we actually go about confession. The Greek word for "confess" in this verse is *homologeo,* which means to "speak the same thing . . . to assent, accord, agree with."[2]

How do we confess sin? We start with an acknowledgement that we are sinners. Then we move on to acknowledge any specific sins for which the Spirit convicts us. In Chapter Three: Questions Answered, we learned in response to "Why did Jesus have to die?" that there is a difference between having a sinful *nature* and committing individual *sins.* Let's be thankful that Christ died for the sinful nature that separates us from Him, and let's be grateful that our forgiveness for specific sins is a sure thing!

Specificity plays a key role in the way we are to confess to both God and people. We will only *experience* God's forgiveness to the level that we are *specific.* I am not referring to whether or not God or another person forgives, but rather, whether or not we *experience* that forgiveness in a way that allows the burden of guilt to be truly gone and allows us to be truly free. A person who says a blanket prayer like, "Lord, I confess that I sinned a lot today. Thank you for forgiving all of it," will experience far less forgiveness than the person who dares to open his or her garbage bag of sin, take out each stinky piece, and show God the whole truth. Letting His forgiveness cover the full stench and filth of each sin we are confessing reassures the *heart* that we really are forgiven.

Some people say, "No need to share the details. God already knows them. Just ask for forgiveness." Please allow me to expound on how to truly reveal the ugliness of our sin so our *experience* of forgiveness is complete.

Scenario #1: Imagine your husband comes into the house at the end of the day and asks, "How was your day?" You respond, "It was hard, honey. The kids were difficult and I lost my temper a few times. (No details are shared.) I'm sorry I wasn't a better mom to our children today. Do you forgive me?" "Sure, honey, I understand. Every day can't be perfect, you know." The evening goes on . . .

Scenario #2: Your husband comes into the house at the end of the day and asks, "How was your day?" You respond, "It was hard, honey. The kids were difficult today and I lost my temper a few times. Let me show you something."

You walk your husband to the trash can and show him the broken plate in the trash. "Honey, I threw this plate across the room. Glass shattered everywhere and one shard barely missed our little boy's face. The kids were terribly frightened and cried for you because they were afraid of me. It was awful! I fell to my knees, sobbing, and hugged them, and we all just sat there in a big mess for a long time. Do you forgive me?" Your husband—having received the full truth—looks you in the eyes and says, "I completely forgive you."

In which scenario will you *experience* greater forgiveness from your husband? In which scenario will you be confident that your husband completely understands the gravity of the situation, but has still forgiven you?

This same principle applies to confessing to God. Of course God forgives us, and He "already knows anyway," but if we are vague in our confession, our *minds* can know we are forgiven, but our *hearts* are not quite so sure. In addition, there's room for Satan to throw us lies if confessions aren't specific. For example, if Satan tries to throw you lies about being a lousy mom for doing such-and-such, you can boldly stand against that lie because you have confessed the full stinky truth aloud and have received God's full forgiveness.

There's a well-known verse you have probably heard:

> For we do not have a high priest who is unable to sympathize with our weaknesses, but we have one who has been tempted in every way, just as we are—yet was without sin. Let us then approach the throne of grace with confidence, so that we may receive mercy and find grace to help us in our time of need.
>
> —Hebrews 4:15–16

The "confidence" Hebrews 4 speaks of is developed over time as again and again we bring the gunk to God. We hold nothing back, and still—even with this mess too—God forgives. Vague confessions keep "shadows" in the heart where honesty is not yet welcome, and blanket confessions don't make us feel clean. Shadows keep us living cautiously and carefully because we still feel guilty and even a bit like a fraud. Until we are ready to let the light of God's holiness shine anywhere it wants to in our hearts, we cannot approach God with confidence.

A sample prayer of confession follows.

The confession part:

> *Dear Jesus,*
> *I confess* ____________ (fill in the blank with specifics and the entire truth) *is sin. Thank You that You died on the cross for this sin too.*

The changing part:

> *I don't want to ever do this again. I now ask the Holy Spirit to fill this area of my life and to empower me to become completely changed.*

Many, many people can say the confession aspect of the prayer with ease. It's the second part at which we hesitate; it is hard to tell God we never want to do it again, and it is hard to tell Him that we are willing to work with Him to see change happen. Do you struggle with this second part? If so, may I gently say this indicates a walled off part of your heart where God is not yet free to go. Be honest about that too. Admit it to God; then see if you can utter the following prayer:

> *Dear Jesus,*
> *I confess that I don't want to change in a way that stops the sin you have shown me. Show me why I am holding on so tightly so I may deal with the root of the problem. Holy*

> *Spirit, invade (name the part of life with which you are struggling).*
> *Amen.*

We now understand *why* we must confess our sins. We cannot have clean hearts, grow closer to God, or be filled with the Holy Spirit without confession. We also now understand *how* we must confess our sins. We need to confess specifically. And we must acknowledge that confession is a two-step process that involves not only agreeing with God that we have sinned, but of also partnering with the Holy Spirit to see sinful parts of our lives transformed. We also need to consider our heart attitudes as we confess sin.

What should our heart attitudes be in confession?

Confession isn't just about agreeing with God that something is sin; it is also about wanting that sin to never live in us again in any way, shape, or form. When we understand the damage sin does to our hearts, we can agree with Oswald Chambers who said, "*. . . it is the greatest moment in my life when I do decide that just as Jesus Christ died for the sin of the world, so sin must die in me, not be curbed, or suppressed or counteracted, but crucified.*"[3]

When we decide that sin must die within us, we let the full work of the cross take place in our lives. Unless we *truly do not want* the sin we are confessing to find a way to live in us again, we are wasting our time confessing it.

Confession is not an exercise of the *mouth*—saying all the right words. It's an exercise of the *heart*, applying the work of the cross to our own hearts and inviting God to rip the sin out of our lives—however He needs to do it. Each of us needs to make sure that when we confess, our mouths speak for what is occurring in our hearts. Otherwise, we are in danger of playing what I call the confession game.

I played the confession game for years, even as I served God faithfully in Christian organizations. In hindsight, I see I wasn't interested in life change at all. I used confession as a way to keep God on my side (or so I thought) when I felt I really needed Him. One area where I played the confession game consistently was in my unhealthy relationship to food. I am guilty of using food as more than enjoyable nutrition and sustenance. I have used food to relieve boredom, calm restlessness, and comfort emotional pain. There were many times when I confessed overeating, not because I was sorry, or saw it as sin, or wanted it gone—but because I had to give a talk to a group of women, and I needed His blessing. When the talk was over, I resumed my unhealthy eating.

Remember how I started this chapter outlining the meaning of Psalm 66:18 and confessing that I have most certainly said *words* of confession without having a *heart* of confession? Psalm 51:17 says, "The sacrifices of God are a broken spirit; a broken and contrite heart, O God, you will not despise." A contrite heart is one that feels or shows sorrow or remorse for a sin or shortcoming.[4] There have been times when my spirit—my heart—has not been broken or remorseful as I confessed my wrongdoings to God. I have not wanted to give up the sins I was confessing. All I wanted was to feel better because I had said the right words. Ha! God was not fooled in the least.

I would say that if you can't remember when you last confessed sin to the Lord, one of the following statements could be true of you.

- You are in a fabulous place with the Lord and aren't sinning much.

- You are failing to consistently examine your heart for sin; therefore, you are not confessing much to God.
- You are confessing with your mouth, but your heart attitude is not sincere, and you do not want to change.
- You are not seeing the sin yet. For example, because I had an immature understanding of sin while I was in college, I was unable to see much of my sin even when I examined my heart. We are all like that in some area of our lives. There are simply things we can't see yet, and that is why we are not confessing them.

What about what I don't know?

In spite of many shallow confessions during the years of my early Christian walk, they still rank as the most visibly fruitful years of ministry in my life. It felt as if all I had to do back then was introduce people to Jesus and they became Christians. I believe my ministry efforts were blessed for two reasons. First, God wasn't blessing *me* when people became Christians. He was blessing the people I was speaking to because their hearts were ready to know Him. All they needed was someone to share how to do that. He can use a rock to get the message of Jesus to people if He wants to, and quite honestly, I was the rock He used at times (Luke 19:40). Second, I simply didn't know. I was not mature. It may not make sense to you, but I loved the Lord with everything I knew love to be at that time in my life. I really did believe that participating in God's story meant being busy doing ministry activities. I really couldn't see the confession game for what it was because my picture of God was small, and I thought He wanted my service first and foremost. Therefore, I believe His grace covered my efforts, as feeble and flawed as they were.

I am comforted by Psalm 19:13, which says, "Keep your servant also from willful sins; may they not rule over me. Then will I be blameless, innocent of great transgression." A willful sin is one that is thought about in advance and done on purpose. If a person is living without sinning on purpose, they are considered "blameless" by God. Blameless does not mean perfect, but rather refers to a person who with a clear conscience is not committing any sins on purpose (Psalm 19:12).[5]

The Bible talks a lot about the value of maintaining a clear conscience. In Genesis, Abraham and his beautiful wife, Sarah, were on a journey and stayed among the Philistines in Gerar. Rather than telling the Philistines that Sarah was his wife, Abraham told them she was his sister. This, unfortunately, communicated to the men of Gerar that Sarah was "available." Sure enough, Abimelech, the king, sent for her. Look at this stunning verse: "Then God said to [Abimelech] in a dream, 'Yes, I know you did this with a clear conscience, and so I have kept you from sinning against me. That is why I did not let you touch her'" (Genesis 20:6).

I have always loved this verse because it demonstrates that in the event that with a clear conscience we simply *don't know* what our sins are, God somehow grants us protection. There is a lot I didn't know during my college years and days of full-time ministry. I am telling you from the bottom of my heart that the Christian girl who was trying to share Jesus with everyone on her college dorm floor had *no clue* she was striving to earn God's love through performance. She had *no clue* she was not capable of miraculous doings in her own strength. She had *no clue* she had a shallow faith.

I. Had. No. Clue.

God protected that naiveté, and used a girl who was doing what she *did know* to do. She shared the message of Jesus Christ with all the people she knew because she cared about their souls. He blessed that.

Please recall the stacks of books that represent our lives in Chapter Eleven: Beginning the Process of Living with a Clean Heart, "The concept of layers." This illustration helps me to understand there is sin in my life today that I can't see. I am committing sins I don't have the maturity to see yet. For example, let's say I confess a sinful behavior like an outburst of anger but do not yet see the faulty thought processes or prideful attitudes underneath that spurred the behavior. Does that mean walls stay in my heart?

Yes, walls are in our hearts. Any area of sin, known or unknown to us, partially blocks God. There isn't a person alive who has attained perfection this side of heaven. However, I believe if we are confessing what we *do* know, God's grace covers what we don't know.

Let's look at 1 John 1:9 again. "If we confess our sins, He is faithful and just to forgive us our sins and cleanse us from all unrighteousness." Notice that if we confess our sins, we are cleansed from *all* unrighteousness. The walls are still there, but they aren't interfering with our relationship with God in the same way they do when they represent sins we are actively refusing to address or confess.

These thoughts comfort me in my relationships with people. I believe that if I am doing all I *have* learned, and I have addressed all the matters He *has* shown me, God will not allow the enemy to use my blind spots for the *ultimate* harm of others. Rather, God will use the struggles I cause in other people for their good. For example, I used to speak in a harsher tone than I do now. I simply couldn't hear it. But because I was confessing all the sins I *did* know about, I trust God used the irritation of my harsh tone to give other people opportunities to practice forgiveness and love. My tone did not ultimately destroy anyone.

We have now discussed many aspects of confession as we have tried to understand it better. It is important that we recognize that we need to apply these aspects of confession not only to our relationship to God, but also in our relationships with others. As we finish out this chapter, we will look at the issue of confessing our sins to others and of forgiving those who have sinned against us.

When do we confess to others?

I do not confess most of my sin to others. Most of the sin God reveals in me is the stuff people can't see such as attitudes and thoughts. Those stay private. When those "invisible" sins rear their ugly heads and show themselves publicly, however, I must confess not only to God, but to the people I have sinned against.

My children once watched a Christian woman have an angry outburst in front of their soccer team. Unfortunately, that same woman never confessed her sin to the soccer team of young girls who so desperately needed her example. I choose to believe that the lady did her confessing to God in private, but I wonder if she understood that she confused the kids who knew she was a Christian. She confused me too! Did she understand that she was a poor role model of how to manage emotions? My general rule of thumb is to confess to those affected by the sin. In this soccer example, it would have been nice if the mom had asked the entire team for forgiveness before or after the next game. If she had asked the children to forgive her, she would have set an example of how to make amends and her relationship with the children would have been restored.

God asks us to go to people quickly when they have something against us. "Therefore, if you are offering your gift at the altar and there remember that your brother has something against you, leave your gift there in front of the altar. First go and be reconciled to your brother; then come and offer your gift" (Matthew 5:23–24).

We are supposed to run to each other when we find out we have offended one another. As lights of the world, we need to treat all of our relationships with utmost care. When our sin mars our reputation, it does the same to people's perceptions about the strength of our relationship with God. We need to clean up the mess for God's reputation as much as we do our own.

What do we do when others sin against us?

"Bear with one another, and forgive whatever grievances you have against each other. Forgive as the Lord forgave you" (Colossians 3:13).

There aren't any loopholes in this verse. Jesus forgave us, so how can we withhold forgiveness from anyone else? It is important to remember that we are all on level ground at the foot of the cross no matter what our level of maturity. All of us have nothing (really) without Jesus. Whatever we have is only a dot.

Think of a time someone wronged you. If the person who wronged you was not a Christian, and thus, had no access to Holy Spirit power, he or she could only operate in the sinful nature. The person was unable to love you and care for you with perfect love. Why do we expect people who do not yet know Jesus to live as if they do know Him? The lost cannot look "found." The broken cannot look "fixed."

Everyone is on level ground at the foot of the cross.

On the lines below the cross pictured above, write your name alongside the name of someone who has hurt you. Spend some time grappling with the truth that from a dot and string perspective, neither of you has anything (really) apart from Jesus.

We are all in relationships with people who sin directly against us. Or their sin may simply splash on us. This "splashing" happens, for example, to the wife of a husband with irresponsible work habits, the mother of a pregnant teen, and the child of parents with a dysfunctional marriage. How do we handle these kinds of things so we can stay clean in the midst of the fallout? Here are six steps to remember as we try to stay clean.

1. Tell God it hurts. (If you don't use a Kleenex for your tears in this step, you may very well be handing God the facts, but not your heart.)
2. Ask the Holy Spirit to take over your heart. Ask Him to empower you to obey and to do the right thing.
3. Confess to God any sins you committed in the scenario. (Keep in mind that when we are hurt by others, we often respond with sin in some way.)

4. Forgive the person who has sinned against you, like Jesus forgave you.
5. Confess your sins to the offender if need be. (Remember, your success is not determined by how the person responds to your confession.)
6. Recognize that in light of eternity, this offense is really just a dot. (You may need to do this before confessing.)

By forgiving those who have sinned against or around us, and by confessing our own part in the sin (if applicable), we take necessary steps for growth to occur in our hearts.

As we end this chapter on confession, it is my hope that you make a decision to pause regularly and examine your heart, the source of all your behaviors, thoughts, and attitudes. Confess and renounce all that God reveals to you. In so doing, God will take full advantage of the room you give Him, and the Holy Spirit will be able to move freely in and through you for His good purposes. By inviting the Holy Spirit to take over our hearts (component 1) and confessing everything God shows us to confess (component 2), we are well on our way in the process of spiritual growth. In the next chapter, we will learn about a third component of experiencing consistent growth no matter what our circumstances.

Chapter Fourteen

Doing Everything You Know to Do

I have now presented two of three components for experiencing optimum growth. The first two components, "Inviting the Holy Spirit to Take Over our Hearts" and "Confessing Everything God Shows Us" were largely accomplished through *prayer*, but not this last one. The third component, "Doing Everything You Know to do" occurs through *obedience*. This chapter explains how to allow the Holy Spirit to empower your *actions* as the final step to produce consistent growth—even in the toughest circumstances.

How do we know what being a Christian looks like when life is difficult? The Bible says to love our neighbors as we love ourselves, but what does that look like at any given instant and with any particular person? What does it mean for the high school student who feels mistreated by a teacher? How does love look for the college student with a difficult roommate? What does love look like for the wife in a difficult marriage who is looking across the breakfast table at her husband? Exactly what is the best way to love the new neighbor who just moved in? What is the best way to love a difficult co-worker? In these situations, where much of life occurs, the black and white pages of the Bible suddenly land on a life that is murky and gray at best.

No one is qualified to tell me exactly what to *do* in order to look like a Christian in this *exact* minute, in this *particular* circumstance. If one of my daughters asks for counsel about how to address an issue with a friend, I have no clue. Of course I pray to speak helpful words, but I preface them by reminding my daughter that in the end, she has to work it out *herself* with the Lord. Only she and God know the sum total of every interaction so far with her friend, the personalities involved, and the network of relationships in which the conflict is occurring. I don't! Only she and God can arrive at the best wording, the optimum time, and the best place to converse.

God made my marriage His best classroom to teach me how to determine what to actually *do* moment-by-moment when life is gray. My relationship with my husband included a long, difficult, complicated season where I couldn't find any pat answers in the Bible. I was honestly stuck in a state of confusion. I didn't have the foggiest idea of what a Christian wife was supposed to look like. There wasn't a shred of me that wanted to leave, but I didn't have a single answer to any of my questions.

One of my dear friends, Sue, walked through that season with me in a way that was life-changing. Instead of giving advice, or sharing her perspective on the events of my life, she taught me a question: "What glorifies God here?" I responded with frustration, "I don't know, that's why I am asking you!" She just patiently answered, "God will show you. Listen for Him."

So I did. I started trying to listen for God's promptings instead of seeking His way for me from outside sources. I started to act on what I thought glorified God by thinking about what would line up with His Word and character. Slowly but surely, I was learning to turn my ear to Him instead of picking up the phone to call my friend. *The battle in our marriage was reduced to just God and me.* I learned a very important principle from Sue. The only thing we can really do for people is point them to Jesus.

For the first time in my life, because God had taken me to a place of desperation, I was listening with a *heart* that was ready to *act.* I was truly postured to live out anything God revealed to me. I developed the desire to become a listening Christian. I wanted my heart to be so soft I would hear even the slightest of God's whispers and then respond.

I have told Sue that her style of counsel birthed the first breath of life into my heart. As you know, prior to this time, I thought walking with God was about living up to a set of external rules and regulations given to us for our protection so we can reap the utmost benefits from God and glorify Him to the greatest degree possible. Suddenly I realized that walking with God was about *resting* in the safety of His love for me and *releasing* Him to do in me and through me what would please His heart the most. This new way of interacting with the Spirit fostered a different kind of relationship with God. I began to live in response to being safely loved instead of operating out of duty.

A word of caution is necessary here. Many people claim they are listening to God and being led by Him. They may say they have a sense of peace about their decisions. But let it be clearly stated here: if something directly violates God's Word, God has no part in it. It is unfortunate that there are Christians who—even while they read their Bibles and pray—leave their spouses and children in order to pursue an adulterous relationship. Any sense of peace they claim to have stems from some source other than God.

Yes, we listen to God, but that ability comes from the work of His Spirit living in us. Every single time, the urgings and promptings we sense must line up with the Bible (what God says),

God's character (what God is like), and God's time table. This way of life called "walking in the Spirit" is the only way to separate ourselves from our sinful nature and to live in His power: "So I say, walk by the Spirit, and you will not gratify the desires of the sinful nature" (Galatians 5:16 NASB). When we get up in the morning, it's not our job to conjure up what to do for the day. Our role is to follow the Spirit's leading.

I once read an analogy about following the Spirit that I have never forgotten. Suppose you become lost while driving somewhere and stop to ask for directions. Instead of describing how to get there, the person says, "Hey, I am going there right now; follow me." You would instantly relax. When someone who knows the way leads us, there is no stress. That's what it is like to walk in the Spirit. Let's get up each morning and set our sights on God. Let's commit to following Him closely all day long. The Spirit knows how to stay on God's heels. He will show us the way.

"The wind blows wherever it pleases. You hear its sound but you cannot tell where it comes from or where it is going. So it is with everyone born of the Spirit" (John 3:8). Since all believers receive the Holy Spirit as a gift when they become Christians, the phrase "everyone born of the Spirit" refers to Christians.

Being Spirit-filled—adopting a lifestyle that is intent on taking every next step the Spirit prompts us to make—produces an exciting life. Just like the wind turns on a dime and switches direction with no warning, God will do the same with people who have their hearts in neutral and allow Him to do the directing from the driver's seat. If you decide to live as a Spirit-filled Christian—no, *when* you decide—get ready. Whatever map you carry in your head about where your life will lead . . . whatever you have dreamed or imagined as the ideal future . . . God will tear it down and build something better.

Your life will become like the wind.

God may lead you to:

- Leave the job you have always known.
- Travel to a country you don't yet know exists.
- Bear children you haven't planned.
- Change your lifestyle in spite of objections from family members.
- Suffer something you don't think you can survive, but you will.

Life can change direction or speed during our next phone call. I have lived that reality and you probably have too. I know the idea of inviting a lifestyle of changed directions is scary, but the Holy Spirit is perfect like God the Father and God the Son. The Spirit lives to glorify the Son, and the Son lives to glorify the Father (John 16:13–15). It is safe to follow His leading. He never makes a mistake and the ramifications of our God-directed actions are guaranteed to produce God-sized results that last for eternity.

When we allow the Holy Spirit to lead:

- That which is black and white becomes Technicolor.
- Miracles will begin to happen.
- You will get to know the safety of His immense love.

Remember, the litmus test of what we really believe is evidenced by our behaviors. Are you hearing the Spirit, but ignoring His nudgings? Are you saying you believe, but are not doing? When I read the lists above, my heart literally aches for that kind of life. I only have a dot to spend, and I want it to count for the string. Let's surrender any preconceptions we have about what life should look like. Let's allow the Spirit to sit in the driver's seat and take us wherever God wishes. In this way, we prove our trust in God with our hands and our feet. We live it out. Other people can help us, counsel us, and pray for us, but this type of life is mainly wrought in the secret places of our listening hearts and doing whatever the Spirit says. Are you letting your hair become wind-blown by the Spirit? Are you doing everything you know to do?

The simple side of doing

When life gets overwhelming for me and I feel pulled in a zillion directions, I often take a deep breath and remember that there are only two things I have to get done on any given day. All I have to do today is please God and go to bed. I don't have to strive to please a husband, four stepchildren, three children, one son-in-law, two step-grandchildren, students, friends, neighbors, employees, and co-workers. When I reflect on the number of people and tasks clamoring for my attention, my head spins. No! I only have to please *one* Person. It makes life simpler. This way of thinking makes me say the following sentences:

- What Laurie tells herself: "Today, I just need to please God and go to bed."
- What Laurie tells people: "Just please God and go to bed."
- What Laurie tells her kids: "If you please God, you will please me."

It's amazing what happens when I revert to what my friend Sue taught me, "What glorifies God here?" Suddenly, the next thing jumps out at me—play with your son, call this friend, hug your husband, water the plants, write that note, pay bills, clean your desk, curl up with God, and read your Bible.

Still at the end of each day, the planner in my phone has a long list of unfinished tasks written in it, but if I can go to bed knowing I did what God asked of me, then I sleep well and in peace. If I just listen to *one* voice each day, then somehow in time, I know *all* will get done. God's will is that I am a good wife, mother, grandmother, teacher, writer, and friend. It will all get done . . . if I listen and then do.

This kind of lifestyle was modeled by Jesus Himself. He was given thirty-three years to change the world for everyone who ever lived, and only three years of it was public ministry. Jesus didn't do what many of us would be tempted to do. He didn't go buy a new planner or gather a committee together. He didn't plan His travel routes and make hotel reservations. He had one simple strategy. He listened to *one* Person and then did exactly what He was told: "For I have come down from heaven not to do my will but to do the will of him who sent me" (John 6:38).

Jesus got up each day of His life, did what His Father asked Him to do, then went to bed. As a result, a way was made for you and me to experience eternal life. Christ came in a human body and proved that the secret of a fruitful life isn't tireless labor or even a long life. It's listening for the Father's voice and acting on what is heard. Why do we do anything differently?

At the end of His earthly life, Christ was able to say to His Father, "I have brought you glory on earth by completing the work you gave me to do" (John 17:4). Acts 13:36 begins with, "When David had served God's purpose in his own generation, he fell asleep; he was buried with his fathers . . ." These verses have prompted me to pray that I would glorify God by completing the work He has given me to do in this generation. Will you join me in this prayer?

I can sometimes allow myself to gain a false sense of being "okay" with God *today* if I intend to make changes *tomorrow.* I will stop yelling at my kids tomorrow. I will pay more attention to my husband starting on our anniversary. I will shop less after the holidays. I will initiate a relationship with my neighbor when the semester ends. Plans and intentions never equal obedience! They are simply games and an indication of blocks in our lives where we are refusing to let God operate *today.*

If we are going to make a difference in this generation, we can't wait until tomorrow to live a Spirit-filled life. Let's all please God *today*—then go to bed.

The difficult side of doing

Sometimes what God asks of me is easy and enjoyable, but the greatest lessons in my life were wrought out of times when doing what God asked was gut-wrenching. Our finest example of how to obey when it is difficult is Jesus Himself as He prepared to face crucifixion. Jesus went to the garden of Gethsemane with His disciples and was sorrowful and troubled. He fell with His face to the ground and prayed, "My Father, if it is possible, may this cup be taken from me" (Matthew 26:39). That is how Jesus the man felt, but Jesus the Son of God revealed what He had already *decided* ahead of time in the next sentence of the verse: "Yet not as I will, but as you will." Christ was praying so earnestly in His anguish that His sweat was like "drops of blood falling to the ground" (Luke 22:44).

Even while He was pouring out His heart about how He *felt* about what God was asking Him to do, His heart was already set to *do* what pleased the Father by accomplishing His purposes. *That* is a heart of obedience.

We will battle with obedience too. I have personally had three of my own "garden surrenders." I have not sweated blood, but I have cried out in anguish, hyperventilated, clawed at the mattress, and sobbed uncontrollably—all the while with a heart that intended to do what the Father was asking me to do.

Garden surrender concerning marriage: As in most marriages, John and I have had seasons of great difficulty in our relationship. One night, I left the house to drive around in the privacy of my car to express some intense feelings about my marriage. I screamed at the top of my lungs and was hoarse for days. Every fiber of my being wanted to leave our house and not go back. But I did go back. I drove up the driveway, entered the house, walked down our hallway while whispering intensely, "I am only doing this for you, God. Only you," and crawled into our bed while staying as close to the edge of the mattress as possible. I can tell you, I returned home that evening for God alone, relying only on His strength, not mine. Today, as I type this very paragraph, John and I have celebrated our twenty-first wedding anniversary. I am so grateful I stayed and continued to *let* God work on both of us. I still believe my return that night was one of my brightest moments for God because it was all for Him. John thanks me regularly for not giving up on him, now that both of us are in a much better place.

Garden surrender concerning children: One night, John's oldest daughter, who lived with us for part of her college education, poured out her heart for two hours on our bed about her childhood after John and her mother divorced. The next morning John and I initiated a court case to gain custody of John's three other children. We flew to another city to begin the court proceedings. While staying in a hotel, I awakened from my sleep, sobbing hysterically and crying out to God, "Don't make me do it!

Don't make me do it!" I sat on a chair by the window while my poor husband had to watch me hysterically pour out my fears and thoughts in prayer about proceeding through the court case that loomed ahead. Kleenex didn't come close to meeting the need. My greatest struggle was over how the ordeal would affect my then elementary school-aged twin girls. After a while, I literally held out my hands to God. I gave Him the pretty little picture I had of what I wanted my children's lives to look like, and I gave Him permission to draw another picture for me instead.

The court battle was everything I feared. It was emotionally draining, financially crippling, and difficult for my young children. In order to stand beside my husband in battle, I had to leave my children for long periods of time and then still be preoccupied with courtroom matters during the time I was with them. They even had to fly to another city and receive a full psychological evaluation. Yet, it is *this* garden experience that has taught me the most about the *safety* of God's story for me. It is *this* garden experience that is most responsible for the understanding I have gained that God's will is *safe.* He will prevail no matter what the motives or character of any other persons with whom I interact.

Our twin girls are now in college and the court case is long behind us. One of them was recently flying over the city where the court case took place. She took a picture with her phone and sent it to her dad. The attached message was that seeing the city brought back happy memories. That text was a miracle. Our lives were ripped open by that court case, but God did indeed protect our children! I am grateful beyond words.

Garden surrender concerning unfair or inconvenient circumstances: While our family was on vacation one year, John's oldest daughter announced that she was pregnant and wanted a wedding in two-and-a-half months. She was immediately forgiven. That was never a question. There were some natural feelings with which to contend, but they were processed rather quickly. Then we had the larger issue of wedding logistics to conquer. In the short time we had to plan a wedding, I had already scheduled neck surgery and a family trip with my parents to Ireland, neither of which could be changed. It also became clear that though I was her stepmother, I would be operating as the mother-of-the-bride in every sense of the term.

My emotions were reeling from the unexpected and overwhelming news of her baby on the way and a wedding to plan. Thankfully, our vacation plan was to stay at a bed and breakfast the next night. Sleeping quarters were separate from the main house. Our children requested that daddy sleep in their quarters so they would feel safe, which allowed me to stay in a quaint bungalow alone. During the night, I woke up from my sleep sobbing yet again. I poured out my feelings and fears, clawed the mattress, and reached for the ceiling as I begged God to help me walk a path that was unfair and inconvenient. Once the tangled emotions were fully expressed, I embraced the situation and asked God to see me through in a manner that would glorify His name.

Now for the miracles. I can tell you my stepdaughter and I didn't have one argument during the entire time we planned the wedding. God allowed us to orchestrate all of our first choices for the church, hotel, and photographer. I had made only one personal request that night in the bungalow—to find a mother-of-the-bride dress in five minutes. I bought the first dress I tried on and it even came complete with a scarf draped around the neck that covered my recent neck-surgery scar!

The greatest miracles, however, occurred after the wedding. At the post wedding brunch, John and I learned about a child in need and raised our hands as being available to raise him. That child is now our son. As for the bride and groom, that quickly planned wedding has now evolved into the sweetest family of four, and all four love Christ. From every angle, amidst what appeared to be unfair and inconvenient circumstances, God was weaving a story that was higher than what anyone could see. Every time I look into the eyes of my young son and the members of my stepdaughter's family, I am so thankful I surrendered to His plan instead of holding onto mine.

Each one of my three garden surrenders was filled with gut-wrenching tears, sobs, private words, and frantic gestures of helplessness. And in each one I determined I was always going to obey my Father. As you can see, He proved faithful each time. I ended up gaining so much of God through each of these valleys that any price I paid paled in comparison. God acquired more room for Himself inside of me as I catapulted to new levels of trust in Him.

Obedience is hard, but without it, we put a halt to further growth and remain hemmed in by the remaining layers in our hearts. God can no longer operate fully within us, and we hinder our ability to reflect His character to the world. Without obedience, we remain in our comfort zones and live lives that can be achieved with mere human effort. We waste our life. Sure, we have a life, but not one that has an eternal legacy because it was lived well for God.

I want God. I want as much of Him as I can get. He rescued me from darkness through Jesus Christ even before I was born or knew I was lost. He offers all of Himself to me every minute of every day. I have full access to His love, strength, wisdom, goodness, and power through the Holy Spirit. Why wouldn't I want to enjoy each one of these blessings? Why wouldn't I want to know, serve and love such a God?

If you have trusted Christ alone for your salvation, invite Him into every aspect of your life. Throw your heart open to Him, keep your heart clean, and take action on anything He shows you to do; but, do make sure that what you think He is showing you lines up with His Word. If it's a nudge to write, a sense to call, an urging to take action, then do it. If you happen to set off on the wrong track by accident, God will somehow make that clear to you. He will not let you continue. God will let nothing interfere with the heart that purposes to be wholly His. "For the eyes of the Lord range throughout the earth to strengthen those whose hearts are fully committed to him" (2 Chronicles 16:9). He longs to reveal Himself to you and will not let you down.

We have spent the last three chapters taking a look at ways in which we partner with the Holy Spirit to see growth take place in our lives. There are three components: *Inviting the Holy Spirit to take over our hearts. Confessing everything God shows us. Doing everything we know to do.*

Chapter Fifteen

Is Our Process ABOVE the Chaos or IN It?

I have concluded each major teaching portion of the book so far by honing in on a particular concern I have for Christians as it pertains to each section's material. In the final chapter of Part Two – Living ABOVE the Chaos, I address my concern as to whether or not the Bible is being held in high regard. When this precious Book is not held in the highest regard it deserves, we are unable to see things from God's vantage point. We inevitably live for dot-sized purposes instead of investing in matters that count forever. In the conclusion of Part Three – Perspective: How Should We View Our Lives?, I present the challenge to assess our perspective—seeing ourselves as God sees us—by examining our behavior. I contend that without strong perspective, we cannot reflect Jesus well to the world.

As I wrap up Part Four – Process: How Do We Live with a Clean Heart?, I will express concerns that we may not be recognizing the key role prayer plays in maintaining a clean and pure heart. Let me review and then explain how prayer fits in.

At the beginning of this "Process" section I asked a question: What would people who have known you for a long time say about your growth as a person? Would they say (1) you are exactly the same as you have always been, (2) you have digressed in character, or (3) you have become more Christ-like with every year? In my opinion, a person's growth process is in chaos if answers one or two apply. In other words, if someone isn't growing, he or she is not living above the chaos, but rather in it.

Unfortunately, I know people who are still exactly the same as they were years ago when I met them. Some of these people serve God hard and love Him well. Yet they remain exactly the same in their internal struggles and approaches to life. In addition, I know people who are worse every time I see them. I am not talking about losing jobs, getting sick, or having family troubles. I am talking about someone that hasn't grown as a *person*. As the years pass by, his or her ability to reflect the character of Christ is either stagnant or diminishing.

Christians aren't supposed to look the same after years of knowing Christ. When Paul addressed the Corinthians about the divisions in their church, he said, "Brothers, I could not address you as spiritual but as worldly—mere infants in Christ. I gave you milk, not solid food, for you were not ready for it. Indeed, you are still not ready" (1 Corinthians 3:1–2). These believers had not lost the seal of the Holy Spirit that secures salvation (Chapter Twelve: Inviting the Holy Spirit to Take Over Our Hearts, "What the Spirit does with our hearts"), but they were lagging in their ability to demonstrate sanctification and holiness. They lacked the maturity that allows us to reflect the character of Christ in the ways we think and behave. I believe only those who do the hard work of keeping their hearts clean and obeying

God can reflect Jesus to the world around them. Our success at doing the work of keeping a clean heart and obeying Christ is hinged directly to the prayers we utter.

Oh, don't get me wrong. We pray. We pray when we are in trouble, when we are happy, and when someone is sick. We are commanded to do all three in James 5:13–15. We also pray for what we want God to do for us, of course. I know this because I hear these prayers. Yes, we are praying. It's the *absence* of some types of prayers that concerns me.

1. Where are prayers for the string?

I wonder how many of us are living for the string. I don't hear prayer requests for eternal matters for months at a time in some of my Christian circles. Where are the prayers about our neighbors needing to know Christ? Where are the stories about how our children's hearts are warming to the message of God? Where are the college students asking us to pray for their roommates' souls? Where are the prayers to send workers to the nations (Luke 10:2)? Where are the tears shed over the same people showing up week after week to worship together and yet demonstrating no growth either as people or a community? Where are our pleas for the string?

2. Where are the prayers to invite?

As noted in this *Process* section, prayer plays an integral role in maintaining a clean heart, which we have learned is the launching pad for growth. It takes prayer to invite God into every aspect of our lives—to throw open the doors of our hearts and lives so that He can come in and do what He wishes!

I wonder how much inviting we are doing because I see so little power, so few miracles, so few surprises, so little change. As we pray, let's invite God into all of our particular concerns and spheres of influence. Let's not dictate to Him the details of how we want Him to operate. We can each say,

> *Lord, I invite you into my relationships (name them), my job concerns (name them), my school (name it), my activities (name them), my dating relationships (name them), my marriage, my neighborhood (name the neighbors), that special event next week, my job search, the friendship I am concerned about, and that vacation we are planning. Have Your way. Cause all the pieces of my life to be integrated into Your perfect story.*

Let's spend more time welcoming His involvement. Once invited, He will rush in and do more than we can conjure in our wildest dreams (1 Corinthians 2:9). I rarely hear those types of prayers anymore. Our lack of surrender-prayers keeps *us* hemmed in and *God* locked out.

3. Where are the confessions?

One reason we may not be throwing the doors of our hearts open is because we feel they aren't worthy of the Holy Spirit's filling. Maybe our hearts are dirty, and as has been discussed, some of us don't want Him to clean us up. In these cases, our growth is stunted and we remain the same, or we get worse. Either way, our growth is in chaos.

When we confess our sins, we pray (1 John 1:9). I am not sure how much confessing is occurring, however. My perception is based on how little I hear people confessing their sins to others and apologizing in a heartfelt manner for their errors. We are commanded to "Confess [our] sins to each other and pray for each other that we may be healed" (James 5:16). I just don't see it happening except when moms are coaching their young children to say they are sorry. Even then, the child is rarely asked to name the wrong—to assent or agree that he or she has sinned.[1] After childhood, confessions of any sort seem to vaporize. Where do they go in the adult world? I don't hear them.

When confession isn't observable in public arenas with people, I wonder if it's happening in our private prayer times with God. This rationale leads me to believe we may not be tending well to our hearts through confession. You might be thinking, "Laurie, just because I am not confessing to people doesn't mean I am not confessing to God." Maybe, but as discussed, the Holy Spirit calls us to restore relationships when we offend (Chapter Thirteen: Confessing Everything God Shows Us, "When do we confess to others?").

If you saw a videotape of the years I was in pain over my brother's death, you wouldn't recognize me. I know, however, that all of the possibilities of such a life still lie in my natural heart. That's why I trade in my heart every day for a new one that is empowered by the precious Holy Spirit. That Spirit is faithful to keep shining an honest light on all the possibilities for evil that are alive in my heart, even if no one else can see them. As I let Him point them out and then confess them quickly, those possibilities get no opportunity to take root or grow. God gets more of my heart bit by bit each year, and because of God's doing, I look more like Jesus.

Are you engaged in the process of having a clean heart so that you can live ABOVE the chaos? If you are, "You will never cease to be the most amazed person on earth at what God has done for you on the inside."[2]

The work of keeping those brick walls from piling up in our hearts is ultimately between each of us and God. As you labor, don't be afraid to break fingernails and to get your hands covered in mortar dust. It's the path to grandeur.

We *are* praying. I know that. I hear the prayers and see the prayer lists. I hear prayers that range from a child's science test to a spouse's cancer. Let's keep it up—and add more. Let's add prayers for the string and pray for people's souls. Let's add prayers of invitation and invite God into all situations to do what *He* wants, not what *we* want. And let's add prayers of confession both to God and people. As glorious as prayer already is, there's room to bring even more glory to God.

Part Five

People: How Do We Get All of This Loving Done?

Chapter Sixteen

Preparing to Love Everyone with God's Love

I mentioned early in the book that the order in which we consider information is as important as the information itself. When our eyes see the perfect, powerful story unfurling above our heads and can see ourselves as God sees us, we gain *perspective.* That perspective fuels the desire to live for the string and to enter into a *process* that enables us to partner with God as He works in our hearts to purify us. Only then—when these elements are in place—do we become capable of truly loving *people* well.

Loving people with an eye toward the string is to be our main concern in this dot of a life. The bulk of our prayer and relational energies should be aimed toward influencing people for the purposes of Christ as our lives converge with lives of others in neighborhoods, jobs, schools, athletics, and friendships. In our homes, we influence people for the purposes of Christ as we foster loving marriages and raise the children of the next generation.

Identifying barriers of loving people

For my entire life, I have longed to love people well; however, I have struggled to do so. Have I cared about their souls? Yes! Have I cared for them as people? Well, maybe not always. I can see now that people often became an item on my checklist of things to "do" for God. In addition, I thought people were ranked, ordered, and separated into categories of value based on such things as success, capabilities, and appearance. My thinking caused interference in my relationships in the form of competition, comparison, and judgment. As a result, I could only love people with my imperfect love rather than with God's love.

Only after embracing the process of growth and providing the Holy Spirit with ever-increasing access to my heart, did God reveal what was preventing me from offering God's love to people. There were three barriers that had produced my paltry and categorizing form of love.

First, I didn't understand I was dead in sin. *Dead.*

"But because of his great love for us, God, who is rich in mercy, made us alive with Christ even when we were dead in transgressions—it is by grace you have been saved" (Ephesians 2:4–5). As embarrassing as it is to admit, I didn't think I was as sinful as other people. I thought I was better than others. It seems I believed other people needed more saving than I did. I was unaware that I believed this until I contemplated what *dead* means. Dead people don't move. Dead people can do nothing for themselves. That is me, were it not for Jesus, along with everyone else on the planet. We all need Jesus to the same degree. Without Jesus we are dead in sin.

Not only did I not understand I was dead in my sin, I did not understand I had been *rescued.* "For he has rescued us from the dominion of darkness and brought us into the kingdom of the

Son he loves, in whom we have redemption, the forgiveness of sins" (Colossians 1:13–14). In order to be rescued, a person has to be in a helpless and unsalvageable situation apart from outside intervention. I thought other people needed to be rescued but that I did not. Oh, sure, I wasn't perfect, but I believed that others had been brought to God in ambulances, while I had walked into God's reception area and wisely signed up for His forgiveness deal. Somewhere along the way I had taken credit for that decision. I finally came to realize that without outside intervention, I would have stayed in my broken state. I am as helpless and in need of Jesus as anyone else on this earth.

Finally, aside from not understanding I was dead apart from Christ and needed to be rescued, I didn't understand that I had been *adopted*. "In love, he predestined us to be adopted as his sons through Jesus Christ, in accordance with his pleasure and will" (Ephesians 1:5). Adopting our son allowed me the experience of doing *all* the work to rescue a child who could do *nothing* to save himself. Ah, the magic word, *nothing*.

The light bulb went off again. I didn't do anything to be adopted into the family of God. God did all the work. I didn't do anything to hear about Jesus at the age of twelve while others had to wait until much later. I can't take credit for knowing Him early in life. Just like He did for every person alive, God did all the work to provide a way of salvation.

Because God restructured my understanding of what salvation means—that apart from Christ I was as dead as anyone else, that I needed to be rescued just like everyone else, and that I have been adopted into His family by His gracious gift—the layer of being judgmental lifted off. God *finally* had a woman whom He could begin to teach to love people. Now when I sense the judgmental monster rearing its ugly head, I think to myself: *If I had that person's DNA and his or her exact life experiences, I would be just like him or her apart from the intervention of God.*

Human beings are amazingly the same! We are all dead in a garbage heap called "sinful nature" until Someone comes along to rescue us and adopt us as His own. When it comes to our need for Jesus and the fact that we can do nothing to earn salvation, the ground is level for people of every culture, skin color, intelligence level, appearance, and personality.

Embracing the command to love people

Once our hearts are prepared to love, we must face the reality that we are expected to love *everyone*. Look at the prelude to the famous verse that encapsulates the Golden Rule. Jesus was asked, "Of all the commandments, which is the most important?" (Mark 12:28) Jesus answered, "The most important one . . . is . . . Love the Lord your God with all your heart and with all your soul and with all your mind and with all your strength. The second is this: Love your neighbor as yourself. There is no commandment greater than these" (Mark 12:29–31).

When asked for the single most important commandment (just one), Jesus answered with two commandments. Notice that Jesus concluded by saying there is no *commandment* (singular) greater than *these* (plural). In other words, no one can love God and *not* love people. And no one can love people and *not* love God. If we love God like we say we do, we must also become lovers of people.

But wait a minute, you may be thinking. There are lots of people who are not yet Christians, but love people! Yes, any person can love others, especially those close to him or her, but that in itself is not God's love. We are told in 1 John 4:7: "Dear friends, let us love one another, for love comes from God. Everyone who loves has been born of God and knows God." Only God's children can share God's love. "We love because He first loved us" (1 John 4:19). All other expressions of love, no matter how stunning and beautiful they appear to be, only influence the dot.

> If you love those who love you, what credit is that to you? Even 'sinners' love those who love them. And if you do good to those who are good to you, what credit is that to you? Even 'sinners' do that. And if you lend to those from whom you expect repayment, what credit is that to you? Even 'sinners' lend to 'sinners,' expecting to be repaid in full.
>
> —Luke 6:32–34

The true test of whether we are extending God's love is if we love people who don't treat us well. When we love people who love us back, we look like everyone else in the world. But when we love people who treat us poorly, the world sees God's love. Therefore, if the world is going to see God's love in us, difficult people *must be* in our lives. In fact, we *need* them in order to be bright lights for God. Without them, the world won't have an opportunity to see God's love through us! With this in mind, we can say, "Thank you, difficult people! Through Holy Spirit power, we are going to respond to you so well that the world will know God's love dwells in us."

Facing the difficulties of loving people

A life devoted to loving people will cost us. There are three things we need to have in place. First, we have to prepare our hearts. God's love has to exist in us, and the Holy Spirit needs to fill us. As discussed in Part Four – Process, allowing God to grow us and clean our hearts is hard work. Once our hearts are ready, actions need to follow. We "do not love with word or tongue but with actions and in truth" (1 John 3:18).

Second, to love for the string means we often don't do what we feel like doing. We are commanded to love everyone, not *like* everyone. Love is a decision we make, a commitment. "Greater love has no one than this, that he lay down his life for his friends" (John 15:13). Jesus literally gave His life for us, but what does laying down our lives look like for you and me? 1 Corinthians 9:19 tells us: "Though I am free and belong to no man, I make myself a slave to everyone, to win as many as possible." Anyone loving people with an eye toward the string makes decisions in light of others, not himself or herself. Such love is sacrificial.

Writing this book for the string has not been easy. Every word I have written has been penned after sacrificing time I could have spent doing something else. Loving my stepchildren for the string has not been easy. I have sacrificed in ways that have prompted people to tell me I have done more than necessary because they aren't "mine." Each Bible Study I have led for the string has required laying down my life. No one sees the effort to prepare the material, clean the house, provide childcare for children, and support each participant in their particular circumstances. I can say along with everyone else who has decided to love people for the string, though I am free to make life easier for myself, I make myself a slave to everyone, to win as many as possible. To those of you who have been "won" to Jesus, you were worth far more than any price I paid.

In addition to preparing our hearts to love and having an eye for the string when we love, we must be willing to contend with enemy interference. Satan is going to recognize Christ followers who have perspective and a clean heart. He will strive to keep them away from anyone who does not yet know Him. Satan will be unsuccessful. Jesus prayed to the Father concerning Christians,

"My prayer is not that you take them out of the world but that you protect them from the evil one" (John 17:15). God will most certainly answer the prayers of His Son, but until He returns, we will contend with Satan's attempts to keep us too busy and distracted to love people.

Those of us who decide to love people for the string need to do the following work: keep our hearts clean; make daily decisions to love even when we don't feel like it; and battle Satan in the midst of hardships. The decision to love people is akin to the decision a soldier makes when he or she volunteers to serve on the front lines. From a spiritual perspective, loving people is like battling on the front lines.

Battles aren't easy to fight, but I gain courage to wage war when I remember each battle has a beginning and an end. The battle to love a difficult neighbor lasts while I live in the same subdivision. The battle to love a roommate lasts for a school year. The battle to love a parent lasts until they pass away. Every relational battle is a dot on the string of eternity. The activities of our enemies, Satan and his demons, are also dot-sized.

That which lasts forever in God's story is God the Father, God the Son (Jesus), God the Holy Spirit, God's angels, God's Word (the Bible), and the souls of people who become Christians. We will enjoy all of these eternal elements of *God's story* forever. I want to spend my dot loving people so as many people as possible can enjoy eternity and live happily ever after. Such a glorious ending for so many people is worth any amount of dot-sized inconvenience or suffering, don't you think?

Let's prioritize people. Let's love everyone at all costs and point people to Jesus. In doing so, will be using our dots to invest in the string.

Finding the people

It's easy to talk about love in a tidy section of a book, but the reality is that loving people isn't tidy. There are things in our hearts that get in the way of loving people. Those need to be removed. Further, we can't pick and choose who we want to love. We are commanded to love everyone. Loving so many people is a difficult undertaking. How are we supposed to get it all done in the midst of our other responsibilities?

Let's see what we can learn from Jesus. Jesus was God, but He was also man and was asked to change the world in his earthly lifetime. We are also asked to take part in God's world changing plans during our brief time on earth. We won't live each day perfectly like Jesus did, but we can learn principles of how to live for the string by carefully investigating Christ's life.

What aspects of Christ's life, which He lived among people, can we emulate? For one, during His life on earth as God-Man, Jesus maintained an intimate relationship with His Father. We can certainly aim to do the same. Jesus also kept close mentoring relationships with His disciples. We too can establish profitable relationships with people whereby we mentor others and are mentored ourselves. Jesus enjoyed friendships with people such as Mary and Martha, a social life that included attending weddings, and a vocation as a carpenter, public speaker, teacher, and healer. We too have friends, engage in social activities, and have jobs.

There are other ways we can learn from Jesus. He didn't meet every need He saw. He left towns without healing everyone who was sick (Mark 6:4–5), and He instructed His disciples to move on when they weren't welcome (Mark 6:11). If Jesus didn't meet every need, it seems safe to assume that we don't need to meet every need in order to accomplish all God asks us to do either. We just need to meet the needs He asks us to meet.

On the cross, Jesus said, "It is finished." And He finished His work without developing a relationship with everyone who had crossed His path. I too just want to finish what God asks of me. If we all do that, everything necessary will be accomplished.

When I feel overwhelmed, I remind myself there is always time to do God's will. Jesus did it. And His life, because it was hinged with the Father, changed the world. Therefore, if I hinge my life to God's, He can use me to change my world. We all live in mini worlds such as college campuses, schools, workplaces, sports teams, churches, neighborhoods, and homes—our lives are loaded with people! God may lead us to different places down the road. However, right now, the list of people we are each called to love is composed of the people we already know.

In this chapter, we looked at heart issues that can get in the way of loving people that I shared from personal experience. We have also examined God's command to love everyone. In addition, we have learned that loving for the string requires hard work, and that God has already placed people in our lives whom He has asked us to love.

In the rest of Part Five – People, we consider how to love our family members, other Christians, and those who do not yet know Christ. At first glance, it may seem that some of the chapters may not apply to you, the reader. I encourage you, however, to read all of the chapters for if the material is not directly applicable for your situation, it may help you to love someone else!

Chapter Seventeen

Loving Children

God's desire for families

From the first page to the last, the Bible is filled with God working out much of His story through families. In the Old Testament God commanded Adam and Eve to have children. He said, "be fruitful and increase in number; fill the earth and subdue it" (Genesis 1:28). Noah and his family were spared in the flood from whom all families since were born. Noah and his sons were also told to "Be fruitful and increase in number and fill the earth" (Genesis 9:1). In the wilderness, only Aaron's direct descendants filled the office of the priesthood (Exodus 28:1). In the New Testament, God sent Jesus into the world as a promised descendant of Abraham (Matthew 1:17) and placed the Savior of the world into a family (Luke 2:4–7, 22–23, 39–40). God commands us to care for families as a priority (1 Timothy 5:8). Perhaps grandest of all, God considers all Christians as members of His "family" (Galatians 6:10, Ephesians 3:15).

God's desire is to use the family structure to teach children about Him (Proverbs 22:6, Deuteronomy 6:4–9). His desire is that each child live for the string by: taking the message of Jesus to all nations (Matthew 28:18–20); displaying lives of strength and beauty no matter what (Isaiah 61:1–3); and being lights of the world (Matthew 5:14–16).

God's desire for parenting

My college-age daughters have noticed the wide range of knowledge people have about Jesus Christ. It stands to reason that children raised in homes where Jesus is talked about and enjoyed as Savior and Lord will know more about Him. Children in homes where spirituality is not discussed or another religion is practiced may know little about Jesus or the Bible. In short, families play a significant role in the spiritual upbringing of a child.

In addition, all families play a large role in the overall quality of life of a child in general. In one class I teach, journals are required. They serve as regular reminders to me that when my children are adults, they will journal about me. I am forming many of the memories they will someday have about their childhood. I am teaching such things as how to view the world and how to manage conflict. No child picked their family or the part of the globe on which they were born. I want to live my life in such a way—and love my children in such a way—that they are thankful that my husband and I are their parents! This is a serious job.

Every day I get up and acknowledge to God that I do not know how to raise my children. I do not know what His plan is for their lives. I do not have the ability to make them turn out well because I do not have power to produce a specific result. I ask Him to do all of that. They are layered individuals, and only God can discern their layers. Life will get messy as God does His construction work to give them a desire for the string and to create Christ-like character in them. I don't know what path each of my children will take in life; therefore, I pray that they will obey Jesus' words spoken in Mark 12:30–31: "Love the Lord your God with all your heart and with all your soul and with all your mind and with all your strength . . . [and] . . . 'Love your neighbor as yourself.'" As life throws them curve balls, I will keep them in God's hands, pay attention to my own responses to them and to God, and pray a thousand times for the end result that they love God and their neighbors the way Jesus commands them to.

Teaching the string

The vast majority of mothers love their children. We care for their physical needs. We dream their dreams. We guide and counsel with countless hours of our time and every ounce of our energy. This chapter isn't about that kind of natural love. This chapter is about loving our children by teaching them God's story, the string.

Before we can parent well for the string, Deuteronomy 6:5–6 has to be true about our relationships with God: "Love the Lord your God with all your heart and with all your soul and with all your strength. These commandments that I give you today are to be upon your hearts." Once that is true of parents, the instructions continue: "Impress them on your children. Talk about them when you sit at home and when you walk along the road, when you lie down and when you get up" (Deuteronomy 6:7).

We love our children for God's purposes when the teachings of God are readily on our lips. When they face problems, we talk about what God says. When they hurt, we extend hugs and prayers. When they plan their lives, we make certain church and youth trips are included. Our job isn't just to keep our children fed and to teach them right from wrong; our job with regard to the string is to teach them about God, His story, and His purposes.

God-ordained authority

God has asked us all to respect our governing authorities.

> Everyone must submit themselves to the governing authorities, for there is no authority except that which God has established. The authorities that exist have been established by God. Consequently, he who rebels against the authority is rebelling against what God has instituted, and those who do so will bring judgment on themselves. For rulers hold no terror for those who do right, but for those who do wrong. Do you want to be free from fear of the one in authority? Then do what is right, and he will commend you.
>
> —Romans 13:1–3

There are many governing authorities in my life of varying degrees—God, police officers, bosses, and my husband, for example. In our home, God is the head of John, John is the head of me (Ephesians 5:25–30, 33), and we are the head of the children (Ephesians 6:1–4), though all the while, I remain under John (Ephesians 5:21–24, 33).

The diagram on the next page shows the order of authority for married couples. (If you have children but are not married, this diagram applies to any person drawing near to God with a clean heart, as discussed in Part Four – Process.)

Notice in the umbrella sketches, children are nestled safely under God, Dad, and Mom. John is not a perfect man. His umbrella has holes in it, as does mine. But when I look up through the holes in John's umbrella, Whom do I see? Yes, that's right. God. And when the *children* look up through the holes of my umbrella and then the holes of John's, Whom do they see? God. When each woman looks through the holes in her husband's umbrella, she sees God's solid umbrella above him. It is only when we step out from under the umbrella of the husband's authority, that we lose the full protection of God's umbrella. Ultimately, God is our husband and protector. "For your Maker is your husband—the LORD Almighty is his name—the Holy One of Israel is your Redeemer; He is called the God of all the earth" (Isaiah 54:5).

For women who are married, because of the umbrella principle, you and your children are safe under your husband's authority *regardless of the state of his relationship with God.* If the wife is walking closely with God, then the children are safe under her protection. Where a wife lacks, the children are safe under the husband's protection. If there is no husband, or the husband and wife both have areas of the same weakness, the children still have God's umbrella of full protection. You can trust this principle for your children. (Please note, if your safety or that of your children is in jeopardy, please seek help. My umbrella illustration may not be the most helpful way at this time for you to view your relationship with your husband or your children.)

Even in a marriage where one spouse is not yet a Christian, God regards the marriage as holy and set apart for His purposes. This extends to the children.

> For the unbelieving husband has been sanctified through his wife, and the unbelieving wife has been sanctified through her believing husband. Otherwise your children would be unclean, but as it is, they are holy.
>
> —1 Corinthians 7:14

If neither spouse is a Christian yet, are children unprotected? Of course most parents love and care for their children, but remember this chapter is about loving children *for God's purposes.* Without God's perspective being sought, without the power of the Holy Spirit, and the knowledge of God's Word and prayer, children miss out on *some* spiritual insight in regard to the string.

Nothing ever interferes with the fact that God is pursuing each person with His love (John 3:16, Acts 17:26–27). The sun came up today so every person in the world has another day to get to know Him (2 Peter 3:9). As we learned in Chapter Eight: As a Soldier, however, Satan is trying to "steal and kill and destroy" (John 10:10). He is trying to keep families and children from learning about how to have an eternal relationship with God. This isn't fun to address, but for me it underscores what is at stake for children when any parent chooses not to accept God's gift of salvation and then draw close to Him with the rest of his or her dot-sized life.

If a wife is *not* in an extreme situation that puts her or her children at risk of physical, sexual, or mental harm, she should not leave God's order of protection over her and her children. If she does so erroneously, the diagram becomes skewed as illustrated on the next page, and a layer of protection is removed from her children.

This diagram can also reflect a marriage between two Christians who are still sharing a home and raising children. Ladies, it is possible

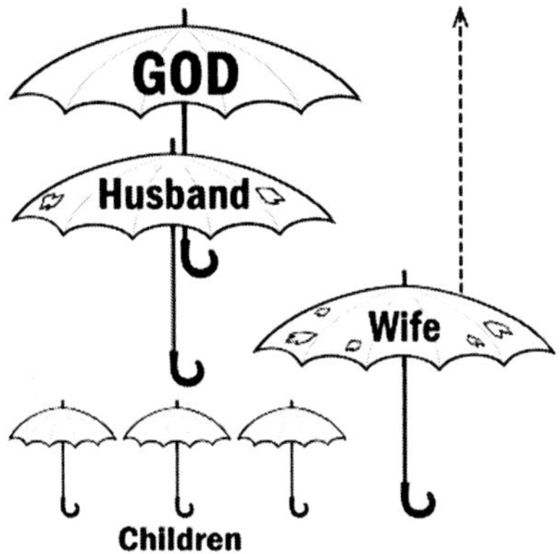

to defy and undermine our husband's authority even when married to a *good* man. I don't know about you, but this diagram motivates me to function in a marriage God's way. I want to die as Mrs. John O'Connor, having done this second marriage well, having crossed the finish line, and having provided for my children the full extent of God's provision and protection by aligning with God's design for marriage.

The skewed umbrella diagram also begs such questions as, "Can we put our children in situations where they do not experience the fullest measure of God's safety?" I believe we can. God has no part in *any* scenario where children are sinned against (James 1:13). Our foster care systems exist to care for children whose parents have not been umbrellas of safety over them. "Is God present with each of those children?" Absolutely! God misses nothing, but He lets parents live by choice, as was discussed in Chapter Three—"Why did God give us choice?"—He is pursuing every child. In the best case scenarios, He heals the parents and restores the family. God also raises up an army of foster care and adoptive parents to offer their homes and love. Finally, He uses the hardships in the children's lives to create a yearning for a relationship with a heavenly Father. But let's not gloss over this. Children are *damaged* by our sin.

John and I are currently certified as resource parents in the foster care system. Through our training, we have learned many foster children have baggage in the form of physical, mental, and emotional damage that makes it harder for them to grasp the love of foster or newly adoptive parents. I believe it also makes it harder for them to grasp the love of a heavenly Father. We don't like to hear it, but the spiritual safety of our children can be affected by our decisions.

This isn't about God's inability to *ultimately* protect a child by using bad situations for their good. It's about God allowing us to choose the ways in which we will love our children. Unfortunately, some of our choices give room for the enemy to gain access to our children. Our choices have high stakes for our children! To think that I play a role in the spiritual protection of my child makes me tremble as even now I head to a little league baseball game. Our little boy needs to be my serious business, and I have to be walking with God to parent him well.

Embrace blended families

Life has always been complicated, but in today's world I see an increase in chaos caused by changes in the family. Steven McCornack says in his textbook *Reflect & Relate*, "60 years ago, the nuclear family—a wife, husband, and their biological or adopted children—was the most common family type in North America. Today, it is in the minority."[1] McCornack continues to explain that any combination of individuals now constitute a family—one or two parents, stepparents and stepsiblings, natural children, and grandparents. Even if parents determine a divorce is best for their marriage, a consequence for the children, for example, might be that they have to split their time between homes, or maybe live with stepparents or additional siblings. Finances are inevitably complicated by such things as alimony, child support, and inevitable financial decisions not addressed in the original divorce papers. The divorced parents experience the added complication of co-parenting with an ex-spouse, or continually dealing with the stress of an ex-spouse who may be difficult. Either way, life is more complicated today for many families than it used to be.

My family shares in the natural complications caused by divorce. John has four children from a previous marriage, which means I have four stepchildren, but that's not the way my heart views them. I live, act, and pray like I have seven children.

Since God views John and me as one (Genesis 2:24; Matthew 19:4–6), as far as I am concerned, I must treat John's children as if they are mine too. My life inextricably becomes one with John's in the eyes of the Lord because we are married. I believe, as a stepmother, that I should see no difference between my natural children and my stepchildren in terms of concern and investment in their lives. For me, it's the same as seeing no difference between the children born to me and a child born to us through adoption.

I know I am speaking to plenty of stepmothers right now, so clarifications are in order. My stepchildren have a natural mother who is fully their mother. I am in no way usurping her position of God-given authority in their lives. Nor am I claiming that I love her children more than she does or even in the same way that she does. What I am saying is that when my stepchildren are in my home or interacting with me, one should not see a difference in the amount of love, energy, and attention I give them as compared to my own children, including our conversations about God. And if someone were to listen in on my prayers on behalf of my stepchildren, he or she would hear no difference in fervency between the prayers offered for my stepchildren and those offered for my own.

God asks us to be peacemakers (Matthew 5:9), and He asks wives not to be quarrelsome (Proverbs 21:9). Therefore, I accept John's children instead of resisting the situation. I want to be an attractive light for Jesus to each of them. I want to trust God with the lives of all seven of our children in the same way John does. I am praying that all seven become a posterity that shines brightly for God after John and I die. Evidence of my faith can be seen by viewing seven initials engraved inside my wedding band and on a bracelet I wear most of the time. There's room on both pieces of jewelry for more letters if God decides to bless us with more children. I include my stepchildren as I pray for God to allow me to leave behind a godly heritage of children that love Him dearly and talk about Him readily. God promises to bless the righteous for a thousand generations, and I am taking Him up on it (Exodus 20:6, Psalm 103:17–18).

At this time, we do not have an amicable relationship with all of the children from John's prior marriage, but I pray for God to chase each of them with His perfect love. If you could view my life as a "reality show" with a voiceover of my prayers, some of what I have asked God for regarding my family would look pretty foolish. On more than one occasion I have said to God, "Lord, what I just prayed sounds so silly compared to my reality, but I am willing to look like a fool for You today, and I want You to know that even if people laugh at me, I believe You can produce life-change in any person or circumstance."

I still may look foolish today, but now I am no longer apologizing to God about my prayers because I have seen enough glimmers of hope and more than a few miraculous life transformations to fuel even more hope into my believing heart. No matter what happens in this big, blended family of ours, a pig-headed stepmom is going to believe God against all odds and continue to pray prayers that sound ludicrous to anyone eavesdropping.

Many of you are in far more complicated situations than I am. God is merciful, patient, and gracious. He will help you through the situation, but please be rigorous in maintaining perspective and a clean heart. If these are not in place, your ability to hear God's promptings will be hindered. Your problems cannot be muscled out with willpower. Only God is qualified to untangle any of your messes; so, have your mind and heart in a condition that allows God to do His work. No matter what your situation looks like, pray like a fool. Believe in God's love for everyone. One of the reasons God made the sun come up this morning is so He can continue to redeem your family.

Chapter Eighteen

Loving Husbands

I have a tender heart for any woman who currently has a husband, once had a husband, or desires to have a husband. No matter your situation, I know your story is complicated. I wish I could write a chapter for your specific situation, but I hope it's evident I comprehend the wide spectrum of scenarios that occurs in the lives of my readers. Since I am currently striving to be an amazing wife the second time around, this chapter is directed mostly at wives. I ask that you search in this chapter for practical applications to your unique circumstances as you are able.

If you are in a situation that seems abusive, this chapter may not apply to you at this time. Please go to a trusted Christian friend or pastor, listen to God with a clean heart to gain His understanding on your circumstances, get professional counseling, and/or call a hotline for help.[1] As you handle your marital hardships, please remember to heed the words of Paul in Philippians 1:27: "Whatever happens, conduct yourselves in a manner worthy of the gospel of Christ." We can be a display of strength and beauty *no matter what.*

For the majority of wives with marriages contained in the very wide category of "normal," if your relationship with God is going well, He will show you how to love your husband no matter what your situation may be. I share below more of my story in the hope that it helps you to love your husband better.

Starting over with my second husband

I have shared enough specific snapshots of my current marriage throughout this book for you to know I have been on a journey in terms of how to be a good wife the second time around. John and I started dating when I wasn't walking with God, and when he didn't know God at all. Our dating relationship had enough drama in it to last a lifetime. By the time our wedding day arrived, however, we were both relating to God well, had just begun a lifelong relationship, and had two babies on the way. Everything was going to be all right. I just forgot a few things. The bride I was in the first marriage was the bride John got in the second marriage. And what took thirty-two years to mess me up—my stack of layers—wasn't going to be cleaned up during a quick engagement and wedding ceremony!

Life got hard again. I still only possessed the same shallow brand of love that I had offered my first husband, and I was only beginning to learn again about how to do life with God. John had his issues as well. So one night—this lady who didn't know anything about how to love someone—did a huge thing. I told God I wasn't going to run this time because I wanted to honor Him and grant Him the room to fix us.

It has not always been an easy ride. I am here to tell you that I made it through some seasons more because of love for God than love for my husband. And I am certain the same is true for him about me. God used the difficult circumstances in our marriage to unearth layers in my heart. As I dealt with each one, my commitment to marriage increased. Mostly, I have come to realize how safe I am in this relationship. My sense of safety stems from the understanding that if I do marriage God's way, God will get the maximum glory from our union as husband and wife, and we will be the brightest lights possible for Him. My life as a wife counts. It has ramifications for eternity; though, I do not yet know what all of them are. God has been faithful to teach me how to love John with His love instead of with the frail love I have to offer on my own. In addition, God has used marriage to deepen my desire to reflect His design for marriage and to participate in His story for my life instead of insisting on writing my own story.

God's design for marriage

In Chapter Seventeen: Loving Children, I proposed that one reason we wives should conduct marriage God's way is for the spiritual protection of our children. I would like to add three more reasons to work hard at being a wife who reflects God's design for marriage.

1. I made a vow.

When I turned forty over a decade ago, I spent some time analyzing my life. Looking back, I realized I hadn't finished much. Meanwhile, God finishes everything. He is faithful. If I am going to reflect His character to the world, I have to faithfully finish things—like my marriage. Relying on God's strength, my word of commitment to John is iron-clad.

2. The world is watching.

> In this same way, husbands ought to love their wives as their own bodies. He who loves his wife loves himself. After all, no one ever hated his own body, but fed and cared for it, just as Christ does

> the church—for we are members of his body. For this reason a man will leave his father and mother and be united to his wife, and the two will become one flesh. This is a profound mystery—but I am talking about Christ and the church.
>
> —Ephesians 5:28–32

Marriage is designed to be a picture to the world of Christ's relationship with the church—all Christians on earth! Christ initiated a relationship with us by pouring out His love upon us. We, in turn, respond with gratitude, adoration, and service to the glory of God! That is how marriage is supposed to work too. Our husbands initiate love; wives respond by loving them in return. Even our physical bodies are designed for the man to initiate and the woman to receive. When the husband loves his wife as he loves himself, the wife responds in kind, and the world gets a glimpse of Christ's relationship to the church. People should be able to learn about the string by watching our marriages.

All too often, however, people do not learn about Christ's relationship with the church by watching Christian marriages, and sometimes wives are a contributing factor. One common error is to compete with our husbands for leadership within the family. After Eve was deceived by the serpent and ate some of the fruit, "she also gave some to her husband, who was with her" (Genesis 3:6). Even though Eve took the lead in that decision, Adam was ultimately held responsible: "For as in Adam all die, so in Christ all are made alive" (1 Corinthians 15:22).

As a result of the first couple's leadership mishap in the garden of Eden, God's specific curse to the woman was to increase pains in childbearing and then He told Eve, "Your desire will be for your husband, but he will rule over you" (Genesis 3:16). Knowing I am tempted to rule over my husband as a result of the curse helps me understand where the "tug" comes from, keeps me from blaming myself, and motivates me not to succumb.

I think we know deep down that if every decision in our homes took place between two spouses vying for the final say, chaos would ensue. Our homes—and the lives of our children—would be destroyed. I am an equal to John, but for purposes of function, someone has to lead.

God will not be asking me to answer for John's role in our marriage, only my role. I don't want to have to tell God someday I not only interfered with John's ability to lead our family, I interfered also with God's ability to illustrate through our marriage how Christ loves the church. Not only is the world watching my marriage, there is a third reason I need to work hard at being a good wife. This reason hits closer to home.

3. The kids are watching.

Not only do I strive to reflect God's design for marriage because I made a vow and the world is watching; I try to do marriage well because the kids are watching. My kids get their most consistent picture of God in our home by watching the way John and I relate to each other. Watching our male-female characteristics meld together into one working unit is a great illustration of God to our children. Through my marriage to John, our children can begin to understand how God can be strong and gentle, holy and loving, just and merciful, and battle-ready and nurturing.

> Wives, submit to your husbands as to the Lord. For the husband is the head of the wife as Christ is the head of the church, his body, of which He is the Savior. Now as the church submits to Christ, so also wives should submit to their husbands in

> everything . . . This is a profound mystery—but I am talking about Christ and the church.
>
> —Ephesians 5:22–24, 32

In addition, as my children watch me prioritize God over John, and then John over them, they learn about order in relationships. When they get married later, they will understand that *with God-given order, everyone gets well taken care of and everything gets done.*

Even though I understand the matters just presented, I still have to contend with the day-to-day realities of living them out, which can be difficult. For example, sometimes John and I don't agree. When that occurs, I strive hard to reflect God's design for marriage for the three reasons presented in this chapter—I made a vow, the world is watching, and the kids are watching. In addition, I strive to honor God in order to maintain the fullest spiritual protection possible for our family.

Handling husband imperfections

Even though John is imperfect, I receive God's fullest protection under his umbrella. If I remain under John's authority, even in the rare instance when he is doing something he knows God does not condone, I am covered. This doesn't mean I won't suffer the consequences of his mistakes. It means that those consequences are ultimately used for my greater good. In God's sovereignty, they will not stop God's best story for my children and me (Psalm 103:17–18).

For example, let's say a husband accepts a corporate relocation for all the wrong reasons and comes home to announce that he is uprooting the entire family and taking them to a new city. The wife handles the announcement about the move well, in a way that glorifies God. Her response looks like this:

- She expresses her full unabridged opinion to her husband without becoming a nag.
- She does the necessary work in her heart to forgive him.
- She makes sure her feelings are shared wisely with God and maybe a few trusted friends who can pray for her.
- She does not share anything negative with the children about their father.
- She trusts God even when she doesn't understand.
- She embraces the new location fully and trusts God that it's her new place on the globe to shine for Him.

I believe a wife who responds like this will not suffer harm. She will experience changes, but only *good* will reign in her life as a result of the move. If that wife continues to trust God and trust her husband's authority, the following is the sort of scenario I would expect *after* the move occurs:

- She suffers the effects of the uprooting associated with the move, but her new location is *better* for God's story.
- She suffers the loss of friends, but the new friends are *better* for God's story.
- She suffers the stresses of forgiveness, but the experience makes her a *better* wife and person for God's story.
- She gains the ability to *better* reflect Christ's character to the world.

> When you pass through the waters, I will be with you; and when you pass through the rivers, they will not sweep over you. When you walk through the fire, you will not be burned; the flames will not set you ablaze.
>
> —Isaiah 43:2

When a husband is making a decision that we would not make, we wives can be tempted to think that our umbrellas are more solid than our husbands'. We might think that we should therefore be making the final decisions. For example, a woman may feel she is more mature in Christ than her husband. Or perhaps, the husband is not yet a Christian. Perhaps the wife thinks she is smarter, more capable, more educated, or more skilled than her husband. Watch out for such thoughts. Any ability I have that my husband does not, I have by the grace of God. I had no control over the family I was born into, the upbringing I received, my genetic make-up, and many of my life's experiences. I therefore cannot lord that over another person like I am somehow better. Add this logic to the spiritual reality that we are all on level ground at the foot of the cross, and I must be careful not to allow any pride on my part to put a wedge in my relationship with my husband. Anything I have is a gift from God to be humbly received and used for His purposes.

Here are some personal examples of how God used John's leadership for my good even when John was making decisions I didn't agree with.

Changing churches

At a time when I was completely satisfied with our church and enjoying a fruitful and exciting season as an adult Sunday school teacher, John grew discontent and wanted to switch churches. I provided him with my unabridged feedback, but in the end, we switched churches and began attending a church we called "Northside." We stayed three years until we moved to a new home.

Guess where the majority of my current best friends come from? That's right, Northside. Four of the women who have overseen the writing of this book—and are named in the acknowledgements—are women I met at that church and with whom I have developed glorious, meaningful friendships.

Our anniversary

For our tenth wedding anniversary, John took me to a Ritz-Carlton for a weekend. I was a polite wife, but I didn't kick up my heels and embrace the weekend with gusto. At the time, I had financial concerns. Since the room at the Ritz was the most expensive one we had ever occupied, I couldn't get the calculator out of my head. I kept fretting about whether or not we had the money. John insisted I get a facial in spite of my spoken concerns about its cost. I got a facial, but I didn't enjoy it. I thought John was being irresponsible with our money and had organized an "over the top" celebration for our ten years together.

We returned home on a Sunday. The following Tuesday, we gained information that led us to begin the heartbreaking, bank-breaking court case I have written about—the one that lasted nine exhausting months and consumed all of our time, energy, and emotions.

I ended up thinking about that weekend at the Ritz quite frequently during the court case. Do you know who gave me the weekend at the Ritz? God did. He knew that two days after my return, my entire world was going to implode and life would never be the same again. God tried to give me a beautiful, extravagant weekend of pampering through John. He knows that sometimes we need to be loved lavishly. After all, God gave us the lavish gift of Jesus! I missed God's gift because I couldn't let John lead. Oh, how I wished I had relished every moment of that luxurious indulgence as the harsh realities of the court case were poised to pounce on us upon our return home. You can bet the next time John takes me to the Ritz, I will allow God to pamper me, and I will enjoy the luxury. I will trust God with my husband's leadership in our marriage.

Now, when John is up for a transfer, or wants to buy a car, or desires to restructure our money, I follow. I have learned that God uses husbands for our good as long as we are not abdicating our responsibility to support and respect them. Staying under our husbands' authority keeps us and our children safely in God's protection.

Chapter Nineteen

Loving While Waiting for Marriage

Since I spend most days with college-aged singles as a teacher and parent, my heart is ripe to speak to single women. I have two burdens on my heart for you as you wait for marriage. First, I encourage you to use your time as a single person to invest in the string. Second, be deliberate in your relationships.

Jesus commands us to "make disciples of all nations" (Matthew 28:19). Looking back, I am so thankful that I used my time as a single person to travel on mission trips to places like Hampton Beach, New Hampshire, the Philippines, and China. Between these trips, I used my time to learn about God through weekly Bible Studies and twice yearly weekend retreats. I spent my social time with close Christian friends. I still cherish those friendships today. For two of my single years, I served with a Christian organization on college campuses in Ohio and Maryland. As I reflect back, I know now that I didn't understand how critical those years were for investing in the string. As busy as I was, it was possible to create more free time then than I can create now with a family.

Now that I am married, the kind of busy I am now is far less *flexible*. Full-time employment has me out of the house for long stretches of time. Children's schedules block my time in large segments. I also can't do anything without the cooperation of four other people. If I want to travel, I must either make arrangements for the three left behind to run things while I am gone, or pay for additional tickets and lodging to take other people along.

All my life I have wanted to build a house with my daughters for Habitat for Humanity and take them on an international mission trip. Each summer came and went as we diligently took a fresh look at the possibilities. Each summer's hopes passed by for a variety of family reasons. Sometimes sports interfered; sometimes John was concerned that the proposed destination wasn't safe; one summer Elizabeth married; other summers, I needed to work. We have just spent two chapters on the key role families play in God's story for the world, but the truth is, families require our time and hinder our flexibility. While you are single, take full advantage of your greater flexibility. Invest in the string by using this time to serve, travel, and learn about God!

In addition, be deliberate in your dating. Begin by considering dating as the process through which people often find their spouse. Do you want a marriage and family that promotes the picture of God to the world? Do you want a spouse whose heart's desire is to raise children who will love God with all their hearts? Do you want a person who handles conflict well? Do you want to be married to someone who is interested in all aspects of his family's well-being, including the spiritual? If you have answered all the questions with a hearty, "yes," as I suspect you have, then I encourage you to do four things.

First, become a person like the one you want to marry. If you want to marry a God-following, Jesus-loving, and Spirit-filled man, make sure you are the kind of woman such a man is seeking to marry—a woman of perspective and process, and a lover of people. In addition, strive for sexual purity from this point onward (Ephesians 5:3, 1 Corinthians 6:18–20).

God had our protection in mind when He confined sex to marriage. Sex while dating can falsely intensify the sense of intimacy one experiences with another person. It can become difficult to decipher whether the other person is really in love with *you* or is merely enjoying the sex. It's also difficult to end a sexual dating relationship. In some sense, you may feel married, and breaking up can feel as earth-shattering as a divorce. Once it becomes clear a dating relationship is not going to lead to the marriage we desire, singles need to be able to move on with minimal heartache. Also, maintaining sexual purity in dating relationships protects marriages from memories that can interfere with being able to focus on and appreciate one's spouse. Premarital sex does not fully satisfy, and it takes something that isn't ours—the purity of the other person that was meant for their future spouse's enjoyment.

If your past contains sexual mistakes, experiencing sex the way God intended is still within reach. Engage in the heart-cleansing process described in Part Four – Process. Then, beginning today, save yourself for your husband. From the night I climbed out of the bathtub and returned to God until the night of our wedding, John and I stayed clear of any sexual activity. Those of us who have not maintained sexual purity can still enter marriage bathed in the purity of God's forgiveness.

In addition to becoming the type of person you want to marry and maintaining sexual purity, be deliberate about your choice of social circles. God can surprise us with our spouse in a chance meeting in the frozen food section of a grocery store, but usually we end up meeting and having relationships with people whose paths we cross regularly either face-to-face or online. Place yourself in environments that fuel your relationship with God and your heart for people to know Him. Utilize personal relationships and social media networks to participate in groups, organizations, and activities that you believe will draw the type of person you want to marry. Be deliberate! Mr. Perfect doesn't exist and neither does the perfect marriage, but choose your spouse carefully so that your future family will have its foundation firmly attached to the string, and you will be able to weather difficult storms when they arise.

Besides becoming the person your dream husband would want to marry, maintaining sexual purity and choosing your social circles carefully, I encourage you to honor your father and mother while you are single and after you are married. Ephesians 6:1–3 is an astounding piece of scripture: "Children, obey your parents in the Lord, for this is right. 'Honor your father and mother'—which is the first commandment with a promise—that it may go well with you and that you may enjoy long life on earth."

Did you notice the promise? Somehow the way you treat your parents is connected to your life's enjoyment. That makes me sit up straight, and I am not even single!

Marriage will limit the time you spend with your parents, so utilize your flexibility and spend time with them now. Grant them respect for what they have done well, and forgive their shortcomings and failures. Honoring parents honors God, as does choosing a godly husband and living for the string rather than the dot. If you do these things, some day you will look back on your singleness and rejoice because you chose to use your single years for Him.

Chapter Twenty

Loving People Who Know Christ Already

> Therefore, as we have opportunity, let us do good to all people, especially to those who belong to the family of believers.
>
> —Galatians 6:10

In every society, it is understood that humans should be committed to their biological families. For example, sport team members and their families understand that attendance at sporting events is mandatory; however, no one would bat an eyelash if a child missed a competition to attend the funeral of a grandparent. Even top-level executives are released from company commitments to run to the side of a spouse when cancer strikes. In the same way we understand commitment to family, Christians should understand commitment to one another. Christians are family members in the household of God (Galatians 6:10, Ephesians 1:5).

Nothing can sever a bloodline. Children are blood related to two parents. Even in adoption and divorces, bloodlines remain acknowledged and permanent. If nothing can interfere with a human bloodline connection, then nothing will sever the family held together by the blood of Christ. My "sisters" and "brothers" in Christ are permanent relatives.

If Christians are viewing our relationships with each other the same way God does, and living as Christ followers, three things ought to be true about our relationships. The first follows:

1. The world should stand amazed as they see our love for one another.

> You are the light of the world. A city on a hill cannot be hidden. Neither do people light a lamp and put it under a bowl. Instead they put it on its stand and it gives light to everyone in the house. In the same way let your light shine before men that they may see your good deeds and praise your father in heaven.
>
> —Matthew 5:14–16

Once we are in the family of God, we not only share dot-kinds-of activities like cooking and tennis, we participate together as a unified light to the world! We have a purpose and mission *together* to live in a manner worthy of the gospel of Christ (Philippians 1:27). We all need to bear responsibility for the reputation of the name of Jesus by not tarnishing His name. Christians should be the most exciting, gracious, kind, confident, relaxed, and loving people on earth. And that should be evident to all who watch us interacting with one another. The world should stand amazed as they see our love for one another.

2. The second thing the world should see is that we have Christian friends.

> For what do righteousness and wickedness have in common? Or what fellowship can light have with darkness? What harmony is there between Christ and Belial? What does a believer have in common with an unbeliever?
>
> —2 Corinthians 6:14–15

If you are a Christian, no matter how much you love someone who doesn't know Christ, that person most likely will not be able to know you as intimately as another believer can. People who do not know God cannot comprehend what touches your heart, drives your actions, and determines how you process events. A wife who is married to an unbelieving husband may love her husband more than her Christian friends, but the *spiritual intimacy* she shares with Christians will exceed that which she experiences in marriage. Christian friends should be able to understand our perspectives on life, join us in activities to encourage mutual growth, and encourage us to live ABOVE the chaos even when we are in difficult situations.

We need to be in relationship with Christians. I know for a fact that many Christians have no solid relationships with other Christians. This is partly because fervent Christians are hard to find. May that change soon! Let's keep searching until we find deep relationships with the people we are going to be interacting with forever.

3. Lastly, the world should see us meeting together.

> And let us consider how we may spur one another on toward love and good deeds. Let us not give up meeting together, as some are in the habit of doing, but let us encourage one another—and all the more as you see the Day approaching.
>
> —Hebrews 10:24–25

Nothing beats getting together with a group of women, sitting in a living room swiftly turning the pages of our Bibles while excitedly sharing information and life applications. I have said that I want to still be leading a home Bible study when I have gray hair and veined hands. That's how I want to go out.

Being in relationship with other Christ followers is a necessary part of our development as individuals and as a community. We need to interact as a family in order to maintain our ability to display lives of strength and beauty to all who are watching.

Like good soldiers, we need to stay in community to live victoriously. Times are going to get tougher, not easier. As the prince of this world gains more room to operate, chaos will increase until one day Christ appears in the clouds.

> For the Lord Himself will come down from heaven, with a loud command, with the voice of the archangel and with the trumpet call of God, and the dead in Christ will rise first. After that, we who are still alive will be caught up together with them in the clouds to meet the Lord in the air. And so we will be with the Lord forever.
>
> —1 Thessalonians 4:16–17

I think about that day. No one knows when that will be. What if I am folding laundry when I suddenly hear trumpets? What if I am teaching class? Whenever it is, I want to be found ready. I want to have an intimate relationship with God and to be found living this dot in light of the string. Either way, whether I am on the earth when Jesus comes or already in the ground, I am going to know one day what it's like to be caught up in the clouds!

It's hard to live as a Christian alone. I am saddened by how difficult it is for my daughters in college to find strong Christian friends who are growing and living for the string. This aching for my daughters isn't just because they are lonely. It runs deeper than that. None of us can stand alone in purity and devotion to Christ against the onslaught of chaos that wants to eat us alive. Any organization—spiritual or not—recognizes the benefits of gathering its members so they can tackle problems together. Have you noticed this? If our collective mission is to live strong and beautiful lives no matter what our circumstances, we need one another.

Our family is currently hoping to adopt a boy from the foster care system, though this may not occur. We periodically peruse photo galleries of children waiting for a "forever family." Christians do not have to wait for a forever family. We have already been adopted into our forever family. That's why we love each other. We are family. So let's love each other well. Let's be strong and beautiful together.

Chapter Twenty-One

Loving People Who Don't Yet Know Christ

As we learned in Chapter Three—"Why are we here?"—we are living in the period of history between Christ's resurrection and His return when He will restore heaven and earth and dwell with His people for all eternity. There is only one thing that cannot occur after the Lord returns. It is that no one else will have a chance to go to heaven. The curtain of opportunity to become Christ followers will have closed.

In addition, this period of history allows us the incredible privilege of having the Holy Spirit reside in every Christian (John 16:7–8, Romans 8:9). On the day of Pentecost, soon after Jesus' resurrection, the Holy Spirit came to dwell inside those who put their faith in Christ. That was not the case in the Old Testament.

> Of God's chosen leaders, we read of only Moses, Joshua, Othniel, Gideon, Jephthah, Samson, Saul and David being touched by the Holy Spirit's presence. Of His prophets the 70 elders of Israel had the Spirit of God on them, as well as Balaam, a

> few messengers of Saul, Amasa, Azariah, Zechariah, Isaiah, and Ezekiel . . . Fewer still were the number in which the Holy Spirit chose to remain.[1]

Because of Pentecost, we should be seeing more power from changed lives than ever before in history. Because God the Holy Spirit dwells in each of us, we can exchange our own strength for His, and we can exchange our sinful nature for His holy one. This should be the era in which our global presence is most strong and beautiful.

Jesus said, "What a huge harvest! And how few the harvest hands. So on your knees; ask the God of the Harvest to send harvest hands" (Luke 10:2, The Message). Any farmer will tell you that harvest needs to take place when the crop is ready, no matter how inconvenient the timing.

During this post-Pentecost period, we should be seeing the greatest gathering of people ever for the kingdom. To aid us in the task of going to all nations—a population exceeding seven billion—the Holy Spirit power of God indwells us. As if that is not enough, the realization that we are living in the last era for people to have a chance to enter God's Kingdom should be producing a sense of urgency in our hearts for the world. I received a typed prayer last week from a fifty-one-year-old friend whose heart holds such urgency: "Lord, use Laurie and I in our relationships this month for Your glory, for the sake of Your Great Name, and for the sake of the unsaved and unreached. Lord, we have about thirty more years to give to you before we are with you forever. Use us for your glory."[2] How many of us have hearts beating in this direction?

The greatest act of love is to introduce people to Jesus. *Our generation is supposed to be offering harvest hands and gathering the lost.*

Everything about our lives should be aimed at participating in reaching the world for Jesus Christ.

The significance of our address

> From one man he made every nation of men, that they should inhabit the whole earth and he determined the *times set for them* and *the exact places where they should live.*
>
> —Acts 17:26, emphasis mine

In Chapter Five: As a Firework, I discussed how God is arranging history like a fireworks display. God launched each of us into the display on the date of our birth, and He picked our spot in the sky by determining our address. We need to understand the significance of our placement in the sky (because of our birthdays and addresses) so we can trust that we live in God's hand-picked places for us. God calls us to love the people living near us.

People don't pick birthdays. God does. Without medical intervention, we can't pick the day a given child is born. Any couple who has struggled with infertility will tell you: babies are a miracle. I am startled when I hear women confidently planning the timing of the birth of their children as if they have any control over the specific paths of sperm and eggs. Regarding the births of my children, God picked the *times set for them*, regardless of the circumstances in which they were conceived. They were all born with me in *this* era of harvest.

Likewise, God picked *the exact places* in which we live. Fifteen years ago, I experienced God's providential placing of my family in a new home. Our prior house sold quickly, and we had twenty-one days to move. We looked at twenty houses in a few grueling days and then narrowed the list to our top five. My husband and I could not have been on more different pages with regard to what we felt we needed and wanted. Besides being in a good school district and in a subdivision, my number one concern was to have a unique piece of property. His number one concern was to have a large master bedroom.

Finally, we had our decisive moment. We stood together on the deck of a home overlooking a backyard. He turned to me and asked, "This yard big enough for you?"

"Yes," I responded. "Is this master bedroom large enough for you?"

"Yes," he answered.

We had our house.

All these years later, no number of books could contain the stories of what has occurred in this house—laughter, tears, growth, family conversations, and gatherings. Our home reflects our personalities in décor, and it's these walls that house our memories. Our children's childhoods took place here, and they will remember this exact spot on the globe for the rest of their lives—this exact address.

But we didn't pick the house. God did.

So why did God pick my birthday and put our family in this exact house for this number of years so far? It has to do with the harvest. Let's focus on Acts 17:26–27 together.

> From one man he made every nation of men that they should inhabit the whole earth; and he determined the times set for them and the exact places where they should live. *God did this so that men would seek him and perhaps reach out for him and find him though he is not far from each of us.*
>
> —Acts 17:26–27, emphasis mine

God has me on this "dirt" on the globe because it is the optimum spot from which I can participate in His story with the people nearby. Our addresses play a large part in determining the people we know. Our addresses determine the schools our children attend, the organizations and teams we join, and the churches we select. The teenagers in my basement this morning from last night's sleepover are in our lives because we live near one another. This is where God has our family, so these are the people with whom I am to be interacting. I can trust that because God picked my address.

I would love to know the well-known Bible teacher Beth Moore personally. But I don't. She lives in Texas, and I live in Georgia. Because God moved me to Georgia, I now rub shoulders with the equally bright lives of people like Jewl, Monica, Sue, and Tish. We all attended the same church at one point. I currently rub shoulders with my favorite Sunday school teacher, Dianne, and all the ladies at my church. God had me in Ohio in 1979 so I could become lifelong friends with Margee; we lived in the same house. God sent me to a Pennsylvania university so I could become lifelong friends with LeAnn; our dorm rooms were adjacent in Holland Hall.

Our place of existence on the globe largely determines the people we are *supposed* to know and love as well as the people to whom we are *supposed* to be a light. The use of social media can shorten distances, and relationships can begin via technology, but most of our relationships are still determined primarily by locale.

God is still in a determined pursuit of every human being. Everyone you know is positioned on the globe so that they "*would seek him and perhaps reach out for him and find him*" (Acts 17:27).

I have an incredibly serendipitous story that builds my trust in God's control over every person's address. Soon after meeting my next-door neighbor fifteen years ago, we discovered she had lived in the *exact* same house I had just moved from. It's true. She and I had lived in the same house in another town prior to becoming next door neighbors in our current town. Though we had lived in the prior house at different times, we had cooked on the same stovetop and washed dishes at the same sink and scrubbed the same toilets. In keeping with this discussion, do you think it's clear that I was supposed to invest in her life and let God do whatever He chooses if He wants to?

One day she knocked on my door and asked if I could be her interior decorator. Did I have time for that? Not really. I was busy. Do I have a degree in interior decorating? No. I just have a knack. Did I need the money? Not at the time.

But I took the job. I had time for *her* because God put her right next to my "dirt," and that was His choosing, and I was going to trust that. I ended up being her decorator for years. She has read my book manuscript more than anyone else and has provided me with extremely helpful feedback. She and I are still as incredibly different as the day I moved in next to her. I have risked it all for her, held nothing back about who I am or who God is. As beautiful as her home is today, our friendship is more beautiful. I love her and suspect our friendship is for life.

The joy of this story is that I didn't make the serendipity happen. The joy of the story is that God picked our birthdays and addresses so that we would live next to each other. God did all of this so that *we would seek him and find him and perhaps reach out for him.* My address matters to the harvest. It determines who I am supposed to tell about Jesus and love with His love.

Our connection to Abraham

Where did this plan begin, the plan for us to collectively be the light of the world? It first began in the garden of Eden with God's "Where are you?" after Adam and Eve sinned. It continued in the stories of Abel, Enoch, and Noah. In the story of Abram beginning in Genesis 11:27, we receive more details about God's plan to use His people to light up the world. Abram was a descendant of Shem, the son of Noah. At that time, almost all people believed in more than one god. Very few worshipped the one true God. Below is a record of his calling:

> The Lord had said to Abram, "Leave your country, your people and your father's household and go to the land I will show you. I will make you into a great nation and I will bless you; I will make your name great and you will be a blessing . . . and all peoples on earth will be blessed through you."
>
> —Genesis 12:1–3

God later told Abraham (whose name had been changed from Abram), "I will make your offspring like the dust of the earth, so that if anyone could count the dust, then your offspring would be counted" (Genesis 13:16). And again He told Abraham, "Look up at the heavens and count the stars—if indeed you can count them." Then He said to him, "So shall your offspring be" (Genesis 15:5). And again, "I will surely bless you and make your descendants as numerous as the stars in the sky and as the sand on the seashore" (Genesis 22:17). Notice the kindness of God to keep repeating not only the promise but also the unbelievable breadth of the promise.

In an e-mail from my seminary-educated friend, LeAnn Bonzo, she stated:

> We know from reading the Old Testament that the Jewish people are the descendants of Abraham in the flesh. Abraham and the Jewish people were chosen by God for a special purpose: to be a

> blessing to "all peoples on earth." This blessing was to take place in two ways. First, the Jewish people were called to shun idolatry and the worship of other gods. They were to worship the one true God so that the people of the "nations" would be drawn to His light. The second way Abraham and his descendants were to be a blessing was through Jesus, the Savior, sent to save the Jews and people from every "nation." Abraham is Jesus' ancestor. God's plan was to rescue the world through Abraham, the Jewish people, and the Savior![3]

When I stand under a starry sky, I can't even begin to count the number of lights scattered across the black expanse of sky. When my children build a sand castle, I can't even see the separate grains, let alone count them. Such *impossibilities* are the numerical *realities* of God's promise to Abraham, who at the time had *no children.*

Mustard seed math is common for God, as we learned in Chapter Seven: As a Mathematician. God told Adam and Eve to "be fruitful and increase in number and *fill the earth*" (Genesis 1:28). God blessed Noah and his sons, saying to them, "Be fruitful and increase in number and *fill the earth*" (Genesis 9:1). He promised Abraham *more* descendants than can be counted (Genesis 13:16). We know from the New Testament that Abraham's descendants include Jews and Gentiles (people from the nations) who have entered into God's family through the same kind of faith Abraham had in God. Paul tells us in Galatians 3:7–9:

> Understand, then, that those who believe are children of Abraham. The Scripture foresaw that God would justify the Gentiles by faith, and announced the gospel in advance to Abraham: "All

> nations will be blessed through you." So those who have faith are blessed along with Abraham, the man of faith.

Take a look at the diagram on the next page. The name Marguerite will be explained later. For now, understand that "If you belong to Christ, you are Abraham's seed, and heirs according to the promise" (Galatians 3:29). When God promised Abraham more descendants than could be counted, He was not just talking about the Jews, the genetic descendants of Abraham (who, according to the New Testament, can only be saved by faith in Christ); He was talking about *all* Christians who would fill the earth from *all* nations and eventually fill heaven! Paul says in Romans 9:8, "In other words, it is not the natural children who are God's children, but it is the children of the promise who are regarded as Abraham's offspring." If you are a Christian, God was talking about you when he spoke of his seed and his heirs.

When you were adopted into God's family, you immediately got swept up into this magnificent promise God gave to Abraham. You became a descendant of Abraham when you became a Christian. You became one of the stars in the sky and grains of sand on the beaches. *Through you* God wants to continue pursuing and growing the number of people who come to know Him and live forever as the redeemed. You can know beyond a shadow of a doubt that God will use you mightily to increase the numbers of people going to heaven, if you let Him, *because He is still keeping His promise to Abraham!*

John 3:16 tells us, "God so loved the *world* that he gave his one and only Son, that whoever believes in him shall not perish but have eternal life." Jesus commissioned Christians to "go make disciples of all *nations*" (Matthew 28:19) and in heaven there will be a great uncountable multitude of people "from every *nation, tribe,*

God's Promise to Abraham

More People Than Can Be Counted
(Genesis 12:1–3, 13:16, 15:7, 22:15–18)

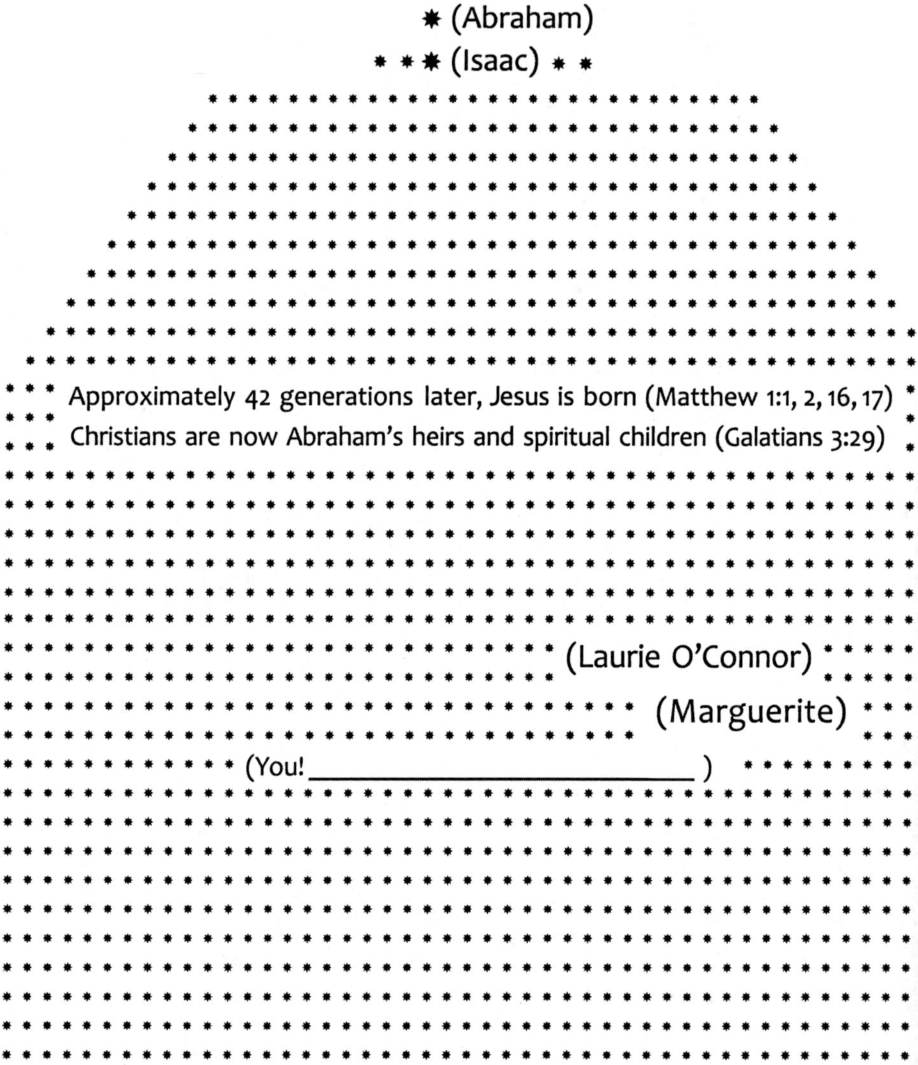

(Abraham)

(Isaac)

Approximately 42 generations later, Jesus is born (Matthew 1:1, 2, 16, 17)
Christians are now Abraham's heirs and spiritual children (Galatians 3:29)

(Laurie O'Connor)

(Marguerite)

(You! ________________________)

Promise to Abraham is fulfilled
Revelation 7:9
"a great multitude no one can count"

people and language" (Revelation 7:9). We are the stars and the sand. We are called to bring others along with us so they can be stars and sand.

Our confidence because of Abraham

If you dare to live transparently and tell people about your relationship with God through Jesus, this promise to Abraham is a 100 percent iron-clad guarantee that God will do great things for Himself and the world through you. Whatever He does with the room you give Him, it will be big.

The first memory I have of taking my light out from under a basket and putting it on a stand was when I was in the seventh grade. I invited my best friend, Marguerite, to an ice cream social at our church, and afterward, we had a sleepover at my house. I wanted to talk with her about Jesus but was afraid. We talked for a while at bedtime and turned out the light. I lay there in the dark, summoning up courage, then asked with trembling hands and a shaky voice if I could turn the light back on and read her a booklet that would explain how to have a personal relationship with God through Jesus Christ. She said okay. The light went back on and twelve-year-old Laurie read a booklet to Marguerite that explained how to have a personal relationship with God through Jesus Christ. It took twenty minutes. Marguerite placed her faith in Christ for the forgiveness of her sins.

That night, heaven got one person larger. What I didn't understand is that I—a seventh grader—had become part of God's promise to grow a nation from Abraham so large that no one could count. Fast forward nine years. I travel to Penn State to attend a gathering of Christians for an evening. One Penn State student shares about her Bible study leader having such a huge role in her spiritual growth. The leader's name? Marguerite. My Marguerite! I hadn't seen her since high school graduation, but look what God had been doing to keep His work going and the numbers growing. I left Penn State understanding that my twenty minutes with Marguerite had been swept up into mustard seed math and had taken on a life of its own because God is still keeping His promise to Abraham.

Fast forward twelve years more and I receive a magazine with a nurse who looked familiar on the cover. Yes, Marguerite. She was featured as a nurse in the Philadelphia area who effectively shares her faith with patients. If she hadn't been the cover story, I never would have known.

Fast forward fifteen more years and I attend my thirtieth high school reunion. Marguerite and her husband are seated opposite me, along with her old high school friend, Chris. Suddenly, Chris leans across the table and asks me, "Aren't you the one that shared Jesus with Marguerite?"

"Yes," I respond.

"I just want to thank you," he said, "because Marguerite shared Christ with me. I shared Christ with my wife and now she and our daughter are both Christians."

I spent the rest of the evening in the company of my spiritual "child," Marguerite, and my spiritual "grandchildren," Chris and his wife. These people are counted as Abraham's descendants; I can trust God with big results because He is keeping His promise to Abraham through Jesus.

I am astounded by what God did with twenty minutes when a twelve-year-old took her light out from under a bowl and put it on a stand for her friend to see. I didn't know my future and all the unseen layers God was going to address and remove, but that night as a twelve-year-old, I was doing everything I knew to do at my level of maturity. My conscience was clear. I didn't know about God's promise to Abraham that night. I didn't know I was an heir to the promise God gave him. I didn't know that when I made room for God to operate, God would rush in and explode that space for His glory. I didn't know a lot that night, except that my friend didn't know Jesus and that I wanted to introduce her to Him since I cared about her soul.

Marguerite is an example of my dot counting for eternity. When the earth passes away, my life's impact on Marguerite, and now Chris and his family, will remain forever. And when my life is over, every decision I have made to give God room to operate in and through me will be rewarded in a way that will impact my eternity, and I will enjoy that reward forever. Living for eternity instead of for my lifetime, living for the string instead of for the dot—this is called living with an eternal perspective.

God didn't have to let me see any of the ways He changed the world with my twenty minutes of time at a sleepover with Marguerite. That was simply His kindness. But if I had never seen her again, the realities of Marguerite's life would still have unfolded without my knowing. It is the same with you. When Abraham died, he had quite a few sons, including Isaac, but "did not receive the things promised." He "only saw them and welcomed them from a distance" (Hebrews 11:13). Look what has happened since. In the same way, when the young man who shared Jesus with me went home that night with nothing to show for his efforts—look what has happened since. He knows nothing about what God has done in me. When you do *anything* to make room for God to operate, you can trust 100 percent that mustard seed math will occur, God's promise to Abraham will surround your efforts, and the harvest will have advanced toward reaching people from every nation, tribe, language, and people (Revelation 7:9).

This is where history is headed in the end (Revelation 21–22). Every person will have been pursued relentlessly by God. Some may question that statement, but Paul declares in Romans 1:20: "For since the creation of the world God's invisible qualities—his eternal power and divine nature—have been clearly seen, being understood from what has been made, so that men are without excuse." I believe the God who had the sun rise again today and is "not wanting anyone to perish" (2 Peter 3:9), will most certainly move heaven and earth to get the specific revelation of Jesus to those who respond to the general revelation of His invisible attributes.

A few years ago, a woman was speaking to our church about ministering to orphans living in sewers in a country overseas. I leaned in to my daughter and said, "Some little boy has been looking at the wonder of the night sky and his heart knows there is a God. Here comes the person who will tell him about Jesus Christ."

Our commitment to people

I recently watched a movie called *The Guardian* about life as a rescue swimmer in the Coast Guard. Not only did the storyline increase my appreciation for men and women who serve our country; it got me thinking about my perspective about people around me who don't know Christ.

Kevin Costner plays Ben Randall, an aging United States Coast Guard rescue swimmer who mentors a young champion swimmer Jake Fischer, played by Ashton Kutcher. Throughout the movie, Jake both admires and competes with Ben. Young Jake is clearly striving to become the Coast Guard's next hero. Throughout the movie, Jake has an incessant curiosity about the number of people Ben has rescued in his stellar career. Jake keeps asking Ben, "What is your number?" and Ben never answers the question until near the end of the movie.

In a late scene, Jake asks Ben, "What's your real number?"

Ben responds, "Twenty-two."

Jake is taken aback, clearly shocked by how low the number is compared to what he thought he would hear.

Because he reveres Ben, Jake says carefully and hesitantly, "Twenty-two?" (pause) "That's not bad. It's not 200 . . ."

"Twenty-two is the number I lost, Jake," interrupts Ben. "It's the only number I kept track of."

Surprise! Jake Fischer and Ben Randall were concerned with opposite numbers, Jake with lives saved and Ben with lives lost.

What would happen if we were to only keep records of those who do not yet know Christ? I have observed attendance being tracked at events, baptisms being tracked, and I have watched people counting response cards and cheering over every positive response for Christ. I have never observed any person watching people walk *out* the door and saying, "Let's get on our knees and pray for all the people who left tonight without Christ. There were twenty-two of them, and that's the only number I care about."

Paul says in Colossians, "For he has rescued us from the dominion of darkness and brought us into the kingdom of the Son He loves, in whom we have redemption, the forgiveness of sins" (Colossians 1:13–14). Now insert your name in the verse and read it repeatedly until it sinks into your heart. "For He has rescued (____________) from the dominion of darkness and brought (______________) into the kingdom of the Son He loves . . ." You were rescued. You were helpless, lost, and drowning in the dominion of darkness.

If I had to pick an earthly situation to help me describe exactly how real my "lostness" was, I would imagine being in an ocean at night, having been left behind after my boat capsized. In the darkness, I am unable to see the next wave coming, so I am continually caught by surprise and my mouth fills with salty water each time the wave comes. I keep choking and sputtering. I am cold and numb and afraid and alone—and I am going to die. Suddenly, a searchlight appears, and a Man comes to get me. I can't do a thing to help myself in my hypothermic state. My Deliverer does all the work. He finds me, secures me in a basket, and I am drawn up into the safety of a hovering helicopter. I am unbelievably rescued, and I am alive.

If you are a Christian, this is what has happened to you. Have you lost touch with that? Perhaps until now you have never comprehended the depth of your past helplessness and despair and hopeless destiny. What if someone hadn't come to find you? You would still be lost and helpless, choking on seawater.

The Bible says, "How then can they call on the one they have not believed in? And how can they believe in the one of whom they have not heard? And how can they hear without someone preaching to them?" (Romans 10:14).

How would your life change if you saw all the people in your life as people in need of rescue? What if you saw yourself as a rescue swimmer? It's a dangerous job for sure, but you are already rescued. Nothing can ultimately be taken from you, so you can risk it all. You are part of God's promise to Abraham. You are a child of the God Who loves mustard seed math. You are filled with the Holy Spirit as a source of power. You have God's Word that never returns empty but always accomplishes what God desires (Isaiah 55:11).

What is stopping you from reaching out to those around you? This segment of history demands a call to action. Jesus has told us to go and make disciples of all nations (Matthew 28:18–20). Christians, where are we?

Francis Chan recently spoke at a *Verge* conference and recounted a simple childhood game most of us have played, *Simon*

Says. A leader would say, "Simon says, 'Pat your head,'" and followers would dutifully pat our heads. Chan then notes, "But it's so weird how in the church . . . if *Jesus* says something, you don't have to do it. You just have to memorize it."[4] Oh, folks, let's not only memorize the verses that tell us to be a light in a dark world. Let's do it, because Jesus says!

I challenge all of us to consistently ask these questions: Are there people in my life who don't know Jesus? Have I fostered enough of a relationship with them to share spiritual matters and answer questions? Am I transparent about my faith in Christ?

Just like something is amiss if we aren't spending time with any Christians, something is amiss if we don't have anyone in our lives *but* Christians. Christian churches and schools are filled with Christians. Social calendars are filled with dates with Christian families. I suspect there are some families not rubbing shoulders with any "darkness" at all, and if they do encounter nonbelievers, it is often by appointment instead of through friendship. An example would be a trip to a rescue mission for two hours and then home again. Our contact stays safely contained in a controllable, scheduled sort of way.

Whatever the reason, we need to rattle our cages and break free. Let's get off the bench and get involved in our society as teachers, political leaders, doctors, purposeful parents, and involved grandparents.

People were created for action, movement, and involvement. On dreary days, we think we want to retire on a tropical island, sitting in a chaise lounge all day facing turquoise water while holding a drink with an umbrella in it. But that is not what we were built for. Adam was given the job of tending the garden of Eden. When God commanded Adam and Eve to "subdue the earth" (Genesis 1:28), He clearly gave them the capacity to do so. Moses and other heroes of the faith engaged in meaningful labor until God called them home. I have a quote on my office wall from adventurer Robert Louis Stevenson: "A ship in a harbor is safe, but that's not what ships are built for." People weren't made to enjoy a safe existence. We come alive only when we are out in the open sea of life and fully engaged as the people God created us to be. I want nothing to do with being a spectator of God's unfolding story. I want Him to fire me into the dark sky and shine His glory in fullest fashion through me.

Our transparency with people

> But in your hearts set apart Christ as Lord. Always be prepared to give an answer to everyone who asks you to give the reason for the hope that you have. But do this with gentleness and respect, keeping a clear conscience, so that those who speak maliciously against your good behavior in Christ may be ashamed of their slander.
>
> —1 Peter 3:15–16

You might be thinking, "I don't know how to help others to believe." I say, "Yes, you do!" Just live transparently. Be who you are. Answer questions honestly. As you live candidly as a Christ follower, someone is going to ask about the Bible study you attend, or ask why you pray, or ask why you like your church, or ask why you are kind to the creepy neighbor, or why you treat your stepchildren so well, or how you can forgive those who hurt you. Even if time is short, give God room to shine through you! Say something, for heaven's sake! Open the door with two things in mind. Bring up the name of Jesus and always end by saying if they ever have any questions, they can feel free to ask. If someone asks a question and you don't know the answer, just say you'll get back with him or her. Ask friends and pastors for help and learn together.

The key is bringing Jesus up and making room for God to operate. Unless you bring up His name, people cannot come to know Him. People can't get into heaven purely by someone "being nice" to them. Nor can they get into heaven by knowing nice people. People find out how to go to heaven if they meet Christians who tell them about Jesus.

> Even though I am free of the demands and expectations of everyone, I have voluntarily become a servant to any and all in order to reach a wide range of people: religious, nonreligious, meticulous moralists, loose-living immoralists, the defeated, the demoralized—whoever. I didn't take on their way of life. I kept my bearings in Christ—but I entered their world and tried to experience things from their point of view. I've become just about every sort of servant to lead those I meet into a God-saved life.
>
> —1 Corinthians 9:19–22 MSG

It's the ache of God's heart that made the sun come up again this morning. Today He is giving every person who doesn't know Him ONE MORE DAY to find Him. He is giving every Christian one more day to tell someone the news of Jesus. I challenge you to be a light, to join in, to be a rescue swimmer, to shoulder the responsibility of living in this era of history. I know that with whatever room you give God to operate; He will rush to fill the space with incomprehensible beauty and mustard seed math.

You may never see the results this side of heaven—but when you hear God describe what He did with your mustard seed faith, it will sound very Abraham-like. The results of your life will be described in terms of stars in the sky and sand on the beaches. Remember Marguerite.

Chapter Twenty-Two

Prioritizing People

I hope by now you want to roll out of bed tomorrow morning and start to make room in your life to be in more effective relationships with people. You are ready to shine! The only problem is, you will still have to work, pay the bills, clean the house, pack the lunches, get kids to school (or home-school them), help your husband . . . well, you get the idea.

Early in my years of motherhood, I contemplated the heavy load of maintenance in my life as I bathed my toddlers one night. I calculated that *in just two short years* of life, I had bathed them together approximately 730 times, tucked them in with prayers individually 1,460 times, purchased and laundered enough clothes to clothe them for 730 days, served 2,190 plates of food, and grocery shopped at least 208 times. That's when it hit me. Most of life is consumed with maintenance, and if I'm not careful, it can keep me so busy I never interact meaningfully with people or God.

Decide to love

None of us can get creative and figure out how to squeeze more people in our lives. That never works. People can sense when they are being squeezed in and nothing profitable will occur. We need to make room. We may not be able to get rid of our jobs, and we certainly can't get rid of our husbands or children. What we can do is streamline our life *maintenance.*

Doing so will take a tremendous amount of effort for the following reasons:

1. *Relationships are difficult because people are difficult:* Because of this, we will be tempted to avoid getting to know new people, or we may walk away when things get hard. In addition, we must persevere in love with difficult people in order to show God's love to the world. Otherwise, we blend in with those who only love people who love them back (Matthew 5:46–48).
2. *The enemy will never allow it to be easy to get together:* In a general sense, the enemy will do everything in his power to erode relationships. More specifically, he will attempt to keep people away from us so they don't have an opportunity to hear about Jesus.
3. *Our culture encourages high maintenance:* American culture is geared toward baubles and beauty, with better cars and nicer clothes. We can only stand against the onslaught if we are joined in force with others, and if we have determined that we want to live an Abraham-like life.
4. *Maintenance has a way of growing:* Have you noticed that? You start to clean a sink and then you notice the drain is clogged. You open a cupboard to get drain cleaner and see that the cupboard needs re-organizing. There goes the afternoon.

Participating in relationships and simplifying maintenance will always be a battle, but we must never allow our motivation to prioritize people to wane. When the dot is luring us to waste time or lose focus on what really matters, please allow the decision to invest in people to prevail.

Decide to streamline

> Therefore, since we are surrounded by such a great cloud of witnesses surrounding us, let us throw off everything that hinders and the sin that so easily entangles. And let us run with perseverance the race marked out for us, fixing our eyes on Jesus, the pioneer and perfecter of faith. For the joy set before him he endured the cross, scorning its shame, and sat down at the right hand of the throne of God.
>
> —Hebrews 12:1–2

We are asked to throw off the sin that so easily entangles. I have already addressed this extensively in Chapters Twelve and Thirteen. But notice that we are *also* asked to throw off everything that hinders—something that is a hindrance or an impediment.[1] The New American Standard Bible uses the word "encumbrance." Sin certainly hinders, but sometimes there are things that exist in our lives that are not sin, but that hinder our ability to run the race of life with endurance. Only you and God know what constitutes a hindrance. For example, a lake house for some Christians is part of God's story for their lives and is used for His glory in the lives of people. For others, a lake house is a financial burden and nothing more than an encumbrance that is sapping the vitality out of the family. Checking for encumbrances is a key aspect of your family's ability to maximize God's glory with your lives. It's not always the *sinful* stuff that renders us ineffective for Christ. Rather, it's the *extra* stuff that keeps us too busy and tired for God and His purposes.

I have known plenty of women who have a huge heart for Jesus. They want to invest in people and long to make room for Him to operate. But they get sucked into caring for the family and home so much that nothing is left for anything or anyone else. They go to bed defeated. *I have been that woman.*

The opposite is also true. I have known women who invest in people to the detriment of their families. Life in their homes is chaotic and their children and husbands need them. I have also seen them go to bed defeated. *I have been that woman too.*

Of course, our families do not interfere in God's story for us. They require maintenance, and plenty of it, but they are gifts from God and our first order of business. Other than that, our reasons for being encumbered differ: jobs, homes, beauty regimens, activities, social media, and shopping; none of which necessarily constitute sins that must be thrown off. It may be the *type* of job, or the *size* of the home, or the *expense* of beauty regimens, or the *number* of activities, or the *hours* utilizing technology, or the *amount* of stuff we purchase that become encumbrances for us. There are books to read on this subject,[2] but I believe the issue as to whether or not these are encumbrances is a personal one that must be resolved between you and God. After all, your life is unique and you make decisions according to *your* particular circumstances.

Sometimes my family members remark about our house as if I picked it. No, our home was chosen after considering the input of all family members and the unique needs of each child, none of which I am obligated to share with everyone, nor could I. It would be impossible to communicate the full gamut of what was going on in our lives at the time—the decline of our prior neighborhood, time constraints of the sale, financial realities, and the marital dynamics that all led to purchasing *this* home as opposed to another. Just like it's impossible for others to know enough to evaluate me fairly within my unique circumstances, it is impossible for me—or you—to evaluate others.

Let's extend grace to each other. Let's urge each other to live for the string and streamline our lives for people, but let's also remember that we *can't* know the intricacies of each person's family life—and we *shouldn't* know everything. Only God does.

Meanwhile, what are we going to do about how we run our own lives? The people in our lives can't hear about Jesus unless someone tells them, and they can't know what Jesus is like unless they interact with someone who exhibits His character. We have a strong and beautiful part to play in God's story, particularly because we live in this segment of history. Let's streamline ruthlessly. Let's purposefully use our time here on earth for people and the string rather than on our belongings, technology, and activities. Someday the thousands of meals we have made, the hours spent at work, and the messages and pictures we have exchanged on social media will be a distant memory, but the people we are with in heaven will be enjoyed forever.

Chapter Twenty-Three

Are Our People Priorities ABOVE the Chaos or IN It?

We have reached our final conclusive chapter of living ABOVE Chaos or IN It? For review, at the end of Part Two – Living ABOVE the Chaos, I shared my opinion that the Bible is not regarded highly enough in Christian circles. In Part Three – Perspective: How Should We View Our Lives?, I challenged us to see if our behavior lines up with how God views us. Part Four – Process: How Do We Live With a Clean Heart? focused on prayer concerns. Here in Part Five – People: How Do We Get All of This Loving Done?, we will discuss my concern that Christians are not rubbing shoulders with darkness, and if we are, we often are not associating ourselves with Jesus Christ.

We are the light of the world, so we need to be around people who don't know Christ yet! Put simply, people who are walking closely with God and talking openly about their faith are living ABOVE the chaos with people. In contrast, believers who do not seize opportunities to talk about Jesus are in chaos with people because they are living predominantly for the dot instead of the string.

I once heard about a man who wrapped his arms around a globe and wept and prayed for all the lost. What evidence do you and I provide about our concern for people who still do not know Jesus, or who do know Him but aren't growing in their relationship with Him? I expressed concern in Chapter Twenty-Two: Loving People Who Don't Know Christ Yet that Christians are not praying enough for the string. As we pray, where are the names? Where are the tears? Where is evidence of an ache for people to know Jesus? I have left church too many times over the years without hearing anyone express concern for people's souls.

Anyone you know today who is not yet a Christian is drowning in a stormy sea right this minute. Without you or another Christian telling him, he or she will die without knowing Christ and live for eternity separated from God. Don't let Satan lull you into thinking people without Christ are doing fine. Or that people with a weak relationship with Christ are doing fine. The hope for all our eternities rests in the strong involvement of Jesus Christ in every area of our lives. Never forget that people who do not know Christ have nothing string-wise.

You may be thinking, okay, Laurie, you stirred my heart. I see my neighborhood differently. I see I am picked to be here. I see my house differently. God picked it. I see the era I am living in as spiritually significant and I am both excited and daunted by the responsibility. But Laurie, I am a student, an athlete, a single mom, a wife, or mother. I work full-time. How am I supposed to donate harvest hands?

Truly, I am right with you on this one. Today, the people in my life include my large immediate family and friends. Add to that all the people associated with my children's lives—the parents and children associated with my children's classes, sports, jobs, and events. Add neighbors in my community, the members of our church, and colleagues at work. Don't forget my extended family like my mom and dad, brother, nieces, and nephews. When all I can see are people taking up my time, or when I want to retreat so even more people don't start taking up my time, I go back to the dot on the string (introduced in Chapter Three—"Why did Dan die early?"). Think about that dot in a new way. View the dot in terms of your spheres of influence and think, *My career is as short as that dot. My time with my children is as short as that dot. My marriage is as short as that dot.* (We will not be married in heaven—Matthew 22:29–30. Our husbands will be our brothers in Christ.) Folks, the things in your lives that people are interrupting are dot-sized. We can let people interrupt our dots for purposes of the string.

Please grab a pencil and turn to the dot and string diagram on page 28. All over the page, write the names of people in your life whom you do not believe know Christ. When you finish, lay your hand on the page and let God know you don't know what to do, but you have figured out one thing. *If you are not purposefully rubbing shoulders with any people who don't know Jesus, something is wrong.* If you aren't near any darkness, you can't shine brightly. If someone in your neighborhood is seeking God, but no one is telling him or her about Christ, God may just have to move that person elsewhere. Have you ever thought about that?

Jesus was criticized for eating with tax collectors and "sinners." On hearing this, He replied, "It is not the healthy who need a doctor, but the sick. I have not come to call the righteous, but sinners" (Mark 2:17). I always marveled that hypocritical religious leaders shunned Jesus, but sinners followed Him and dined with Him, rather than staying away. I wonder why. I wonder since He saw the layers and knew exactly why each person was the way they were, He interacted perfectly with each one and no one felt judged. Rather, each felt known and experienced perfect love from a Man who introduced the concept of eternal life to them.

As God-loving, Jesus-following, Holy Spirit-filled people, we can hope to be a light like Jesus who attracts people. We need to be around people in order to live like that; however, let us each say with John Keith Falconer, "I have but one candle to burn and would rather burn it out where people are dying in darkness than in a land which is flooded with lights."[1]

Chapter Twenty-Four

It's Time to Rise Up and Shine!

> Today's mighty oak is just yesterday's nut that held its ground.
>
> (Author unknown)

It's a scary thing to write a book. In essence, this book is a "freeze frame" of who I am as of today, but tomorrow, I will already be different. I will tweak this manuscript daily until it is submitted for printing, and the morning after it is turned in, I will want to edit something else and won't be able to do so. Please allow me to grow beyond each of the thoughts addressed in this book. Learn what you are supposed to learn from these pages and then surge ahead into knowing so much more about God that this book becomes outdated. People change, but God and His Word never will—we will enjoy both forever.

Dan's death was a tragedy for me—and everyone agrees to that. Some people even say they understand why I "went off the deep end" for a season. I, however, cannot concur with such thinking. Remember, I was a Christian before Dan died. That title calls me to a higher response to life's events. God the Father pursued me through history (as He does everyone) and established me firmly in an eternal relationship with Him through His Son Jesus Christ. I am also sealed by the presence of the Holy Spirit of God Who lives inside of me. God, Who spoke the world into existence and calls the stars by name, is my heavenly Father. Therefore—as with all Christians—I should live a life of incredible strength and beauty.

I remain crushed that I did not live up to the name of "Christian" when my brother died, and did not honor God with my response to tragedy. I confused people who knew me. I hadn't been just Laurie the friend or family member. I had been Laurie the *Christian.*

As I sorted through my own pain, I found answers for many age-old questions, which now provide me greater stability while living in the midst of chaos. Allow me to review them below:

- *Why did Dan die early?* He didn't. No one dies early when one sees each life span confined to a dot as compared to the string of eternity.
- *Why is God not to blame for Dan's death?* Death came with the curse. It did not originate with God. The curse killed Dan.
- *Why did "the curse" happen to all people?* God is holy; so, He can't ignore sin. Our broken spiritual condition is passed to us along with our physical DNA. God is also love; so, He makes a way for us to have an intimate relationship with Him again through Jesus.

- *Why did Jesus have to die?* Three reasons: We need a Savior. He had to break the curse of death. He was the only Person qualified for the job.
- *Why did God give us choice?* Without choice, love cannot exist.
- *Who is Satan?* A fallen angel with limited and temporary power.
- *Why is Satan permitted to operate today?* So he doesn't operate in our eternity (the string). His activities stay contained in a dot. God has allowed Satan's brief reign to continue so everyone on earth who does not yet know Christ will have another opportunity to receive Him and to have eternal life.
- *How is God in control of this chaos?* First, God's larger story in history is undeterred by chaos. Second, chaos is sifted through His fingers for our ultimate good. Third, our response is critical. If we *let* God use the suffering for our good, we participate in God's victory by displaying His strength and beauty to the world.
- *What decisions face each of us?* Are we going to trust God with this brief dot of a life so we can participate in His eternal string? Are we going to trust Jesus *alone* for our salvation? Are we going to trust Jesus—the One who died for our sins and then rose again—to break the curse so we can live forever?
- *Why are we here?* To be bright lights in a dark world.

Oh, how I hope seeing these questions and answers in one place provides a cohesive sketch of what God is up to with history.

With those thoughts tucked into place, let's review the three big ideas discussed in the book.

Perspective: How Should We View Our Lives?

I hope your eyes see differently now. I hope you are exhilarated at the thought that you play a significant role in history. That role is to reflect the character of Christ to the world through the power of His Spirit—to be a display of strength and beauty no matter what. Relax in the truth that God has always been in control of this chaos, and He always will be. You can confidently place your dot of time into His capable, loving hands and live for the eternal string.

Process: How Do We Live With a Clean Heart?

Don't be afraid of allowing God to clean your heart. Don't be afraid of being honest about anything God shows you that isn't holy. His searchlight for the shadows in your heart is always welcome news. You will know His forgiveness personally if you don't run from the truth, and you will see such exponential growth that you will turn around at some point in the future and ask slack-jawed, "Who is this person I have become?" She's strong in the Lord and displays His beauty!

People: How Do We Get All of This Loving Done?

More specifically, how do we love with an eye toward the string? People are our business in this segment of history. It's harvest time. Let's love everyone we meet. Whoever you happen to be with—God has been in relentless pursuit of him or her, and now He is asking you to be a part of that pursuit. We are all on level ground at the foot of the cross. We all equally need Jesus. If we can remember that we have been rescued from the same sin we see in others, it will be easier to love the people in our lives.

Since loving people is to be our major focus in life apart from our personal relationship with God, we need to make room for people so we can love them! Shed the encumbrances. Rid yourself of that which hinders. Let us all ask the Lord to show us how to live more simply so we have room in our dot to live for the string!

People well-rooted in
God's perspective and growth process
inevitably commit to a lifestyle of
loving people and sharing Christ.

Only when Christ followers develop deep roots that allow for consistent growth and live visibly as followers of Christ can we become the light of the world we are intended to be. My passion to see such faith displayed among all Christians around the globe has led me to launch *Oaks Ministries.* I hope to inspire people to exhibit strong and beautiful faith the world can see. I also want to come alongside and assist with laying the groundwork necessary for faith to grow.

Oak trees are strong because they grow slowly, and are not easily toppled by what occurs in their environment. They are also beautiful. A mature oak is often considered magnificent, especially when compared to the acorn seed from which God grew the tree. Considering these characteristics, I desire faith like an oak tree.

Perhaps you too are inspired to develop such faith, but now what? I suggest you have a "marked moment" with God. This is my own term that describes major decision-making moments I have had with God.

One such moment I have described is the night in the hotel room where I sobbed because I didn't want to involve my sweet little girls in a complicated court case. I *literally* lifted my cupped hands into the air and "handed" God the pretty little picture I had for my children's lives. I marked the moment. Although I haven't been perfect, I have essentially *kept* my children in His hands—not fretting over every problem they face and supporting their dreams even if I will miss them when they go away.

I strongly encourage each of you to mark a moment with regard to what God has done in your heart as a result of this book. If it helps, on the last page of this book, I have compiled a list of key concepts, and have placed them in a prayer format that you can pray aloud. Set up a specific time when you can concentrate and select a place that is special to you. The key is to make a *deliberate* decision that you can remember. Whatever ends up being your heartfelt prayer—whether spoken or written—I suspect that like me, you won't be perfect after the moment of decision, but evidence of your decision will always be apparent in your life.

Let's lift our eyes to the stars like God asked Abraham to do. Let's understand that God will use our dot of a life for grand purposes if we let Him have His way with us. Let's live ABOVE the chaos, refusing to get sucked into the affairs of this brief life. Let's be the light of the world with the kind of light God intended for us to be. Let's shine:

- with a *strong* light, one that continues to shine regardless of the circumstances,
- and with a *beautiful* light, one that is worthy of His name.

> In the same way, let your light shine before men, that they may see your good deeds and praise your Father in heaven.
>
> —Matthew 5:16

A Prayer of Commitment to God

Dear Lord,

Now that I understand better that . . .

- I did nothing to deserve hearing about Jesus (Romans 10:14).
- I have nothing without Jesus, and am on level ground with every human being at the foot of the cross (Ephesians 2:4–5, 8–9; Colossians 1:13–14).
- The chaos I experience is contained in a dot of time so brief that the last blink of my eye represents its brevity (Psalms 39:5).
- Eternity is safe, and You are guarding it with cherubim and a flaming sword as I read this (Genesis 2:9, 16–17; 3:6–7, 22–24).
- Satan's power is limited and short (Revelation 12:12; Mark 1:34; Job 1:12, 2:6; James 4:7).
- I can spend my time in heaven doing many things except for telling more people about Jesus (2 Peter 3:8–10; 1 Thessalonians 4:16–18).
- "Tomorrow" all of this is over, and I will truly live happily ever after (Revelation 21, 22:1–5).

I give you the dot of my life.
To the God Who asked me to exchange my dot for the string,
I surrender my life today in order to be used for
Your purposes instead of mine.

Name______________________________ Date __________

Endnotes

Chapter Three

1. This idea is from the writings of Joni Eareckson Tada.
2. Charles Caldwell Ryrie, "The Doctrine of Angels," in *Ryrie Study Bible: New American Standard* (Chicago: Moody Press, 1978), 1943.
3. David Platt, "9Marks at Southeastern," published December 19, 2012, http://www.youtube.com/watch?v=JZ0X_crtytE (June 20, 2013).
4. Lehman Strauss, "The Doctrine of Sin." http://bible.org/article/doctrine-sin (June 12, 2013).
5. Joni Eareckson Tada, taken from *Pearls of Great Price* (Michigan: *Zondervan, 2006); Joni and Friends Daily Devotional* (March 3, 2012 entry), http://www.joniandfriends.org/daily-devotional/.
6. David Platt, "9Marks at Southeastern," published December 19, 2012, http://www.youtube.com/watch?v=JZ0X_crtytE (June 20, 2013).
7. Oswald Chambers, *My Utmost for His Highest* (1935; repr. Michigan: Discovery House, 1963), July 26 entry.
8. Ibid., May 8 entry.
9. Charles Caldwell Ryrie, "The Doctrine of Angels," in *Ryrie Study Bible: New American Standard* (Chicago: Moody Press, 1978), 1943.
10. Ibid., 1944.
11. Ibid., 1943.

12. Tony Evans, *The TRUTH about ANGELS and DEMONS* (Chicago: Moody Publishers, 2005), 8.
13. Ibid., 11.
14. Joni Eareckson Tada, *Heaven: Your Real Home* (Michigan: Zondervan, 1995), 170.
15. Tony Evans, 40–41.
16. Joni Eareckson Tada, taken from *Pearls of Great Price* (Michigan: Zondervan, 2006); *Joni and Friends Daily Devotional* (September 24, 2011 entry), http://www.joniandfriends.org/daily-devotional/.
17. Philip Yancey, *Prayer: Does It Make any Difference?* (Michigan: Zondervan, 2006), 325–326.
18. Beth Moore, *Esther: It's Tough Being a Woman* (Nashville: LifeWay Press, 2008), Video Session 1.
19. Beth Moore, *A Woman's Heart: God's Dwelling Place* (Nashville: LifeWay Press, 2008).
20. Priscilla Shirer, *Gideon: Your weakness. God's STRENGTH*, (Nashville, Lifeway Press, 2013), Video Session 7.

Chapter Four

1. Josh McDowell, *Evidence that Demands a Verdict: Historical evidences for the Christian faith*, revised edition (San Bernardino: Here's Life Publishers, Inc., 1979).
2. Ibid., 16–17.
3. Ibid., 17.
4. Ibid.

Chapter Five

1. Mary Poplin, *Finding Calcutta* (Westmont, IL: IVP Books, 2008), 94.
2. Priscilla Shirer, *Gideon: Your weakness. God's STRENGTH*, (Nashville: LifeWay Press, 2013), Video Session 2.

Chapter Six

1. Edward W. Goodrick and John R. Kohlenberger III, *Zondervan Exhaustive Concordance,* 2nd ed. (Grand Rapids: Zondervan Publishing House, 1999), 422, 1469.
2. Joni Eareckson Tada, *A Quiet Place in a Crazy World* (Colorado Springs: Multnomah Books, 1993), 157–159.

Chapter Eight

1. Stasi Eldredge, *Captivating* (Nashville: Thomas Nelson, 2005), 199.

Chapter Eleven

1. Oswald Chambers, *My Utmost for His Highest* (1935; repr. Michigan: Discovery House, 1963), March 18 entry.

Chapter Twelve

1. *ESV Study Bible* (Wheaton: Crossway, 2001), 2286.
2. W. E. Vine, Merrill F. Unger, and William White, Jr., *Vine's Complete Expository Dictionary* (Nashville: Thomas Nelson, 1996), 545–546.
3. Ibid., 545.
4. Ibid., 546, "Saints" (verse 9) and "believers" (verse 41) translated from *hagios.*
5. Ibid., 545.
6. Ibid.
7. LeAnn Bonzo, e-mail Friday, June 21, 2013, 2:05 p.m.
8. Charles Caldwell Ryrie, "The Doctrine of the Holy Spirit," in *The Ryrie Study Bible* (The Moody Bible Institute of Chicago, 1978), 1941.
9. Ibid., 1939.
10. Ibid., 1940.
11. The Holy Spirit is equally associated with God in Acts 5:3–4; Matthew 28:19; 2 Corinthians 13:14. Like God the Father, the Spirit

knows all (1 Corinthians 2:10–11), is present everywhere (Psalm 139:7), and is all-powerful (Genesis 1:2).

12. I learned this concept from Joni Eareckson Tada, *Heaven: Your Real Home* (Grand Rapids: Zondervan Publishing House), 38.
13. Sheila Walsh, *Good Morning, Lord: I Don't Know Where You're Going Today But I'm Going with You* (Nashville: Thomas Nelson, 2010), cover.

Chapter Thirteen

1. *"The Treasury of David: Psalm 66:18," Bible Study Tools* (May 6, 2013), http://www.biblestudytools.com/commentaries/.
2. W. E. Vine, Merrill F. Unger, and William White, Jr., *Vine's Complete Expository Dictionary* (Nashville: Thomas Nelson, 1996), New Testament, 120.
3. Oswald Chambers, *My Utmost for His Highest* (1935; repr. Michigan: Discovery House, 1963), April 10 entry.
4. *Merriam-Webster Online: Dictionary and Thesaurus,* http://www.merriam-webster.com/contrite (May 6, 2013).
5. Beth Moore, *A Woman's Heart: God's Dwelling Place* (Nashville: LifeWay Press, 2008), Session Six DVD.

Chapter Fifteen

1. W. E. Vine, Merrill F. Unger, and William White, Jr., *Vine's Complete Expository Dictionary* (Nashville: Thomas Nelson, 1996), New Testament, 120.
2. Oswald Chambers, *My Utmost for His Highest* (1935; repr. Michigan: Discovery House, 1963), March 23 entry.

Chapter Seventeen

1. Steven McCornack, *Reflect & Relate*, 3rd ed. (Boston: Bedford/St Martin's), 325.

Chapter Eighteen

1. 1-800-799-SAFE (7233), *The Hotline*, accessed March 8, 2013, http://www.thehotline.org/.

Chapter Twenty-One

1. Beth Moore, *A Woman's Heart: God's Dwelling Place* (Nashville: LifeWay Press, 1995), 63.
2. LeAnn Bonzo, e-mail message to author, May 5, 2013.
3. Ibid.
4. Francis Chan, "Francis Chan: Simon Says," published January 1, 2013, speaking at Verge conference, http://www.youtube.com/watch?v=BibuOmp-dhY.

Chapter Twenty-Two

1. Edward W. Goodrick and John R. Kohlenberger III, *Zondervan Exhaustive Concordance,* 2nd ed. (Grand Rapids: Zondervan Publishing House, 1999), 527, 1575.
2. Jen Hatmacker, *7: an experimental mutiny against excess* (Nashville: B&H Publishing Group, 2012); Jeff Shinabarger, *More or Less* (Colorado Springs: David C Cook, 2013); Matthew Sleeth, MD, *24/6: a prescription for a happier, healthier life* (Carol Stream: Tyndale House Publishers, Inc., 2012); Sign up to receive garage sale alerts in your area on www.ayardsalesearch.com (accessed August 7, 2013).

Chapter Twenty-Three

1. John Keith Falconer, "Evangelism and Revival Quotes," *Tentmaker*, accessed June 24, 2013, http://www.tentmaker.org/Quotes/evangelismquotes.htm.

About the Author

Laurie is the founder of Oaks Ministries. Professionally, she has spent decades working in fields of communication—such as training and teaching, writing, and speaking. Laurie has lived in both rural countrysides and cities, and has worked for both an hourly wage and a corporate salary. The twists and turns of life have led her to Georgia where she currently resides with her family.

This book contains the information I would share with someone who wanted to firmly establish a meaningful relationship with God from the ground up. For me, the information is as important as the order in which I have presented it: Perspective, Process, and *then* People. May God now produce the growth that allows you to be a unique display of His strength and beauty to the world (1 Corinthians 3:6–7). I pray you have been inspired to *Live ABOVE the Chaos* no matter what.

Laurie O'Connor

Founder, *Oaks Ministries*

Website and blog: www.oaksministries.com

Twitter: @oaksministries

E-mail Laurie at laurieoconnor@oaksministries.com